Teatime SAVORIES

BEEF-MUSHROOM CARBONNADE IN
PASTRY SHELLS
page 46

PORK & MOLE CROSTINI
page 98

APPLE, HAZELNUT & CACAO NIB
TRIPLE-STACK TEA SANDWICHES
page 82

Teatime
SAVORIES

A cherished collection of time-honored recipes

83 press

83 press

Copyright ©2025 by Hoffman Media

All rights reserved. No part of this book may be reproduced or transmitted in any form or by any means, electronic or mechanical, including photocopying, or by any information storage and retrieval system, without permission in writing from Hoffman Media. Reviewers may quote brief passages for specific inclusion in a magazine or newspaper.

Hoffman Media
2323 2nd Avenue North
Birmingham, Alabama 35203
hoffmanmedia.com

ISBN #979-8-9913469-9-3
Printed in China

ON THE COVER:
(Front Cover) Earl Grey Chicken Salad Tea Sandwiches, page 61; Chilled Sweet Pea Soup, page 24; [tiered stand] Arugula-Pecan Pesto & Goat Cheese Tea Sandwiches, page 72; Asparagus-Topped Frittata Bites, page 42; Champagne & Tarragon Radish Flower Canapés, page 107; Curried Shrimp & Mango Salad Tea Sandwiches, page 67. (Back Cover) Cucumber-Herbed Cheese Tea Sandwiches, page 62.

CURRIED EGG SALAD CANAPÉS
page 97

PROSCIUTTO & ARTICHOKE HERBED CROSTINI
page 97

HONEY HAM & DIJON TEA SANDWICHES
page 76

SMOKED SALMON & CAPER CREAM CHEESE–FILLED CUCUMBER CANAPÉS
page 102

MINI ZUCCHINI QUICHES
page 34

Contents

INTRODUCTION 8
TEA-STEEPING GUIDE 11
TEA-PAIRING GUIDE 12

RECIPES

COMFORTING SOUPS 14
SCRUMPTIOUS QUICHES & PASTRIES 30
TASTY TEA SANDWICHES 58
DELECTABLE CANAPÉS & CROSTINI 90
MISCELLANEOUS SAVORIES GALORE 116

USEFUL RESOURCES

ACKNOWLEDGMENTS 132
RECIPE INDEX 134

Introduction

THE SAVORIES COURSE FOR AFTERNOON TEA CAN SOMETIMES BE RATHER PREDICTABLE, with dainty, fingerlike sandwiches filled with cucumber, chicken salad, smoked salmon, or egg mayonnaise (salad) occupying a level of the tiered stand. But as the recipes in this curated collection from the test kitchens of *TeaTime* magazine will attest, the iconic course can comprise an exciting array of visual presentations as well as creative twists on traditional favorites. Savvy hosts enjoy varying the offerings from tea party to tea party to include an assortment of tastes and textures—crunchy crostini and luscious frittata bites, among others. Warm dishes, such as soups and quiches, can transform afternoon tea into a tea luncheon or a proper high tea, depending on time of day. A perusal of the five chapters in this tome is sure to tempt the taste buds, pique curiosity, and yield a bounty of inspiration for future teatimes.

    It is fitting to acknowledge that there is debate among tea lovers concerning when the savory foods should be served during afternoon tea. In the British tradition, they are served first, followed by scones and desserts. In contrast, some tearooms in North America and elsewhere prefer to offer warm scones with lashings of clotted cream and jam as the first course, savories second, and sweets to finish. Whichever order is more desirable can be intensely personal or situational but should always be met with grace and gratitude.

    To assist thoughtful hosts who wish to accommodate guests' allergies and aversions, the recipe index (page 134) is organized by primary ingredients and calls out offerings that are completely gluten-free. Guides for properly steeping tea and for determining which teas to serve with which foods are found on pages 11 and 12, respectively, and will be undoubtedly important in assuring that each guest will savor every sip and morsel, making the teatime oh-so memorable.

CARAMELIZED LEEK & PANCETTA QUICHE
page 33

DATE & ROASTED CHICKEN SALAD TEA SANDWICHES
page 66

SMOKED SALMON BLINI
page 108

TEA-STEEPING *Guide*

The quality of the tea served at afternoon tea is as important as the food and the décor. To be sure your infusion is successful every time, here are some basic guidelines to follow.

WATER

Always use the best water possible. If the water tastes good, so will your tea. Heat the water on the stove top or in an electric kettle to the desired temperature. A microwave oven is not recommended.

TEMPERATURE

Heating the water to the correct temperature is arguably one of the most important factors in making a pot of great tea. Pouring boiling water on green, white, or oolong tea leaves can result in a very unpleasant brew. Always refer to the tea purveyor's packaging for specific instructions, but in general, use 170° to 195° water for these delicate tea types. Reserve boiling (212°) water for black and puerh teas, as well as herbal and fruit tisanes.

TEAPOT

If the teapot you plan to use is delicate, warm it with hot tap water first to avert possible cracking. Discard this water before adding the tea leaves or tea bags.

TEA

Use the highest-quality tea you can afford, whether loose leaf or prepackaged in bags or sachets. Remember that these better teas can often be steeped more than once. When using loose-leaf tea, generally use 1 generous teaspoon of dry leaf per 8 ounces of water, and use an infuser basket. For a stronger infusion, add another teaspoonful or two of dry tea leaf.

TIME

As soon as the water reaches the correct temperature for the type of tea, pour it over the leaves or tea bag in the teapot, and cover the pot with a lid. Set a timer—usually 1 to 2 minutes for whites and oolongs; 2 to 3 minutes for greens; and 3 to 5 minutes for blacks, puerhs, and herbals. (Steeping tea longer than recommended can yield a bitter infusion.) When the timer goes off, remove the infuser basket or the tea bags from the teapot.

ENJOYMENT

For best flavor, serve the tea as soon as possible. Keep the beverage warm atop a lighted warmer or under your favorite tea cozy if necessary.

TEA-PAIRING *Guide*

Choosing a tea that perfectly complements the menu for afternoon tea is a critical part of hosting a successful event. When selecting infusions to accompany savory morsels, keep in mind that the taste of the tea should enhance—rather than compete with or overpower—the flavors and mouthfeel of the food, and vice versa. For that reason, we recommend reserving delicate teas, such as the whites, for drinking on their own. Greens, blacks, puerhs, and many oolongs are excellent choices for serving alongside the savory teatime course. The following guide offers recommendations of teas to pair with the various flavor profiles of many recipes in this book, but it should by no means be considered definitive:

CHEESE (MILD) Golden Tips Assam Black Tea, Ceylon Blackwood Estate Black Tea, Nepal Monsoon Black Tea

CHEESE (STRONG) Da Hong Pao Oolong Tea, Golden Monkey Black Tea, Gunpowder Green Tea

EGGS & POULTRY Goddess of Mercy Oolong Tea, Dragonwell Green Tea, Darjeeling 2nd Flush Black Tea

FRUIT Taiwan Jade Oolong Tea, Darjeeling 1st Flush Black Tea, Oriental Beauty Oolong Tea, Vietnamese Black Tea

RED MEAT Ceylon UVA Highlands Black Tea, Grand Keemun China Black Tea, Russian Caravan Black Tea

SALAD & VEGETABLES Young Hyson Green Tea, Keemun Spring Mao Feng Black Tea, Japanese Sencha Green Tea

SEAFOOD Gyokuro Green Tea, Tung Ting Oolong Tea, Ceylon Lover's Leap Black Tea, Darjeeling Autumnal Flush Black Tea

SMOKED MEAT Imperial Yunnan Black Tea, Assam Black Tea, Irish Breakfast Black Tea

SPICY Imperial Puerh Special Grade, Ceylon Highlands Black Tea, Tippy Yunnan Black Tea, Organic Assam Belseri Estate Black Tea

A prudent host will prepare the chosen tea in advance of the event to verify that the pairing is pleasing and to determine the most beneficial water temperature and steep time. This will ensure good tea and a delightful teatime. For a list of purveyors of fine teas such as these, turn to page 133.

CHILLED
SWEET PEA SOUP
page 24

COMFORTING
Soups

FROM CREAMY AND VEGETABLE-FILLED TO HERBACEOUS AND HEARTY, THESE SATISFYING SOUPS ARE SURE TO PLEASE.

remove center piece of lid to let steam escape; place a clean towel over opening in lid to avoid splatters. Blend until smooth.
• Just before serving, garnish individual servings with bread cubes and fresh thyme, if desired.

KITCHEN NOTE:
For a gluten-free version of this soup, use a gluten-free broth and omit bread cubes.

Carrot-Apple Soup
Makes approximately 8 (½-cup) servings

This delicious soup, laden with vegetables and fruit, provides a warm and nutritious addition to the savories course for afternoon tea.

2 tablespoons unsalted butter
1 cup diced sweet onion
1 teaspoon minced garlic
½ cup thinly sliced celery
1 teaspoon fine sea salt
½ teaspoon chopped fresh sage
¼ teaspoon ground red pepper
¼ teaspoon ground black pepper
¼ teaspoon grated fresh ginger
1 (32-ounce) carton vegetable stock
2 cups finely diced carrot
2 cups finely diced Honeycrisp apple
¼ cup heavy whipping cream
Garnish: celery leaves

• In a medium Dutch oven, melt butter over medium heat. Add onion and garlic; cook until fragrant, approximately 3 minutes. Stir in celery, salt, sage, red pepper, black pepper, and ginger; cook, stirring frequently, until celery is translucent, approximately 3 minutes. Stir in stock, carrot, and apple; bring to a boil. Reduce heat, and simmer for 30 minutes. Stir in cream, and simmer for 10 minutes. Let cool slightly.
• Using a handheld immersion blender, carefully blend hot soup until smooth.
• Garnish individual servings with celery leaves, if desired. Serve immediately.

MAKE-AHEAD TIP: Soup can be made up to 3 days in advance; stored in a shallow, airtight container; and refrigerated until needed. Reheat gently before serving.

Golden Beet Soup
Makes approximately 16 (½-cup) servings

Golden beets, lemon juice, and fresh herbs produce this pretty and sumptuous soup.

2 tablespoons unsalted butter
2 tablespoons walnut oil
10 medium golden beets, peeled and chopped
3 cups chopped yellow onion
1½ tablespoons minced garlic
2 (32-ounce) cartons low-sodium vegetable broth
½ cup heavy whipping cream
1½ tablespoons fresh lemon juice
1 tablespoon minced fresh thyme
1½ teaspoons minced fresh parsley
1 teaspoon fine sea salt
1 teaspoon ground black pepper
Garnish: toasted bread cubes and fresh thyme

• In a large stockpot, heat together butter and oil over medium-high heat. Add beets, onion, and garlic, stirring to combine. Cook until vegetables soften, 8 to 12 minutes.
• Stir in broth. Simmer for 20 minutes.
• Stir in cream until well incorporated. Stir in thyme, parsley, salt, and pepper. Cook until heated through, approximately 6 minutes. Remove from heat, and let cool slightly.
• Working in batches, if necessary, transfer soup to the container of a blender. Secure lid on blender, and

Soupe à l'Oignon
Makes 6 (⅝-cup) servings

French onion soup (Soupe à l'Oignon) is timeless for a reason, and this version will become your new favorite. Serve with Asparagus and Ham Tartines (page 108), as pictured, or savor it on its own.

3 tablespoons unsalted butter
2 cups chopped sweet onions
1 teaspoon finely chopped garlic
1 bay leaf
1 sprig fresh thyme
½ teaspoon fine sea salt
¼ teaspoon ground black pepper
½ cup red wine, such as Cabernet Sauvignon
1½ tablespoons all-purpose flour
3 cups beef broth
Buttered Croutons (recipe follows)
1 cup coarsely shredded Gruyère cheese
Garnish: snipped fresh parsley

- Preheat oven to 350°. Place 6 (6-ounce) heatproof ramekins on a rimmed baking sheet.
- In a medium saucepan, melt butter over medium-high heat. Add onions, stirring to coat with butter. Stir in garlic, bay leaf, thyme, salt, and pepper. Reduce heat to medium-low; cook, stirring occasionally, until onions are very tender and lightly golden brown, approximately 15 minutes. (If onions begin to brown, reduce heat.) Remove bay leaf and thyme sprig.
- Add wine. Increase heat to medium, and cook until wine evaporates. Stir in flour; cook for 3 to 5 minutes, stirring occasionally. Stir in broth, and bring to a simmer. Cook until flavors are melded, 10 to 15 minutes.
- Divide soup among ramekins. Top soup with Buttered Croutons and cheese.
- Bake until cheese melts, approximately 5 minutes.
- Garnish with parsley, if desired. Serve immediately.

Buttered Croutons
Makes 2 cups

These homemade toppings for Soupe à l'Oignon come together quickly and will make you never want to serve store-bought croutons again.

2 cups cubed French bread
2 tablespoons unsalted butter, melted

• Preheat oven to 350°. Line a rimmed baking sheet with parchment paper.
• In a medium bowl, toss together bread cubes and melted butter. Scatter buttered bread cubes in a single layer on prepared baking sheet.
• Bake until bread cubes are golden brown, 7 to 10 minutes, stirring if necessary to brown evenly.

Cauliflower-Leek Soup
Makes approximately 24 (½-cup) servings

For winter fêtes, this luscious combination of sliced leeks, garlic, cauliflower, and potato is quite delectable and is heartier than it looks.

3 tablespoons olive oil
3 cups thinly sliced leeks (approximately 2 large leeks)
5 cloves garlic, mashed
8 cups cauliflower florets (approximately 1 large head)
2½ cups chopped, peeled russet potato
6 cups vegetable stock
1½ teaspoons fine sea salt
1 cup heavy whipping cream
Garnish: chopped fresh chives

• In a large Dutch oven, heat oil over medium heat. Add leeks, and cook, stirring occasionally, until tender, approximately 5 minutes (do not brown). Stir in garlic, cooking until fragrant, approximately 1 minute. Stir in cauliflower, potato, stock, and salt. Bring to a boil; reduce heat, cover, and simmer until tender, approximately 20 minutes. Remove from heat and let sit, covered, for 20 minutes.
• Working in batches, purée together cauliflower mixture and cream in blender until smooth. Serve hot.
• Garnish individual servings with chives, if desired.

Tomato-Basil Soup
Makes approximately 12 (½-cup) servings

A heartwarming classic is a fitting addition to the savories course of afternoon tea, especially for Christmas. Add a touch of whimsy by topping each serving with a homemade star-shaped crouton. Soup is pictured with Baked Ham and Cheese Sliders (page 79).

1 tablespoon extra-virgin olive oil
⅓ cup sliced shallot
2 (28-ounce) cans whole peeled tomatoes
¼ cup coarsely chopped loosely packed fresh basil leaves
¾ teaspoon fine sea salt
⅛ teaspoon ground black pepper
⅓ cup heavy whipping cream
1 teaspoon granulated sugar
Garnish: Star Croutons (recipe follows)

• In a large saucepan, heat oil over medium-high heat until oil shimmers. Add shallot, stirring and cooking for 1 to 2 minutes. Reduce heat to low, and cook shallot until tender, stirring frequently, 3 to 4 minutes. Add tomatoes, crushing coarsely with a potato masher or large spoon. Stir in basil, salt, and pepper. Bring soup to a boil, then reduce heat, and cover pan with lid slightly ajar until soup simmers gently. Cook soup, stirring occasionally, for 45 minutes.
• Remove pan from heat. Stir in cream and sugar. Using an immersion blender, blend soup until very creamy. (Taste and adjust seasonings, if necessary.) Serve warm.
• Garnish individual servings with Star Croutons, if desired.

MAKE-AHEAD TIP: To allow flavors to meld, soup can be made a day in advance, placed in a covered container, and refrigerated until needed. Reheat gently before serving.

Star Croutons
Makes 12

Although we used white sandwich bread, homemade croutons are simple to make with virtually any type of bread. We used a 1½-inch cutter shaped like a star, but other shapes would also work.

3 slices firm white sandwich bread, frozen
1 tablespoon unsalted butter, melted
⅛ teaspoon sandwich seasoning*

• Preheat oven to 350°.
• Using a 1½-inch star-shaped cutter, cut 12 stars from frozen bread slices, discarding scraps.
• Gently toss bread stars in melted butter, covering evenly.
• Lay bread stars in a single layer on a rimmed baking sheet. Sprinkle lightly with sandwich seasoning.
• Bake until bread stars are lightly browned and evenly crisp, 7 to 10 minutes, flipping bread stars halfway through baking time. Let cool completely.

*We used Penzeys Sandwich Sprinkle, which is a dry blend of salt, garlic, black pepper, basil, oregano, rosemary, thyme, and marjoram, available at penzeys.com or by calling 800-741-7787.

MAKE-AHEAD TIP: Star Croutons can be made up to a day in advance and stored in an airtight container.

Curried Red Lentil–Carrot Soup
Makes approximately 16 (½-cup) servings

Carrots, red lentils, and curry powder lend gorgeous color to this satisfying soup. An added bonus is that it's vegan.

2 tablespoons olive oil
1 cup chopped shallots
½ cup chopped celery
2 tablespoons tomato paste
2 teaspoons minced garlic
2 teaspoons minced fresh ginger
1 teaspoon curry powder
1 teaspoon fine sea salt
½ teaspoon ground black pepper
1 cup coarsely chopped carrot
1 cup dried red lentils, rinsed, and picked over
3½ cups vegetable broth, divided
1 (13.5-ounce) can full-fat coconut milk
2 teaspoons red wine vinegar
Garnish: coconut yogurt and fresh cilantro

- In a Dutch oven, heat oil over medium-high heat. Stir in shallots and celery; cook until translucent, approximately 5 minutes. Stir in tomato paste, garlic, ginger, curry powder, salt, and pepper; cook for 1 minute. Stir in carrot; cook for 5 minutes. Stir in lentils and 3 cups broth. Bring mixture to a boil. Reduce heat to low, and let simmer until vegetables and lentils are tender, approximately 25 minutes, adding remaining ½ cup broth, if needed.
- Stir in coconut milk and vinegar. Let cool slightly.
- Working in batches, if necessary, transfer soup to the container of a blender. Secure lid on blender, and remove center piece of lid to let steam escape; place a clean towel over opening in lid to avoid splatters. Blend until smooth.
- Garnish individual servings with yogurt and cilantro, if desired.

Mascarpone-Broccoli Soup
Makes approximately 12 (½-cup) servings

This rich soup has brilliant creaminess and tang from mascarpone cheese and a delightful crunch from homemade Leaf Crackers.

7 cups coarsely chopped fresh broccoli florets
¼ cup sliced shallot
1 (32-ounce) carton low-sodium chicken broth
½ cup mascarpone cheese
¼ cup heavy whipping cream
1 teaspoon fine sea salt
Garnish: Leaf Crackers (recipe follows)

• In a large saucepan, combine broccoli, shallot, and broth. Bring to a boil over high heat. Reduce heat to low, and cook, covered, until broccoli is tender but still light green, approximately 10 minutes.
• Remove from heat. Stir in cheese, cream, and salt. Using a handheld immersion blender, process until smooth and creamy. Serve warm. (If necessary, reheat gently over low heat.)
• Garnish individual servings with Leaf Crackers, if desired.

Leaf Crackers
Makes 12

It only takes three ingredients—piecrust dough, egg, and water—to create the charming topping for our Mascarpone-Broccoli Soup.

½ (14.1-ounce) package refrigerated piecrust dough (1 sheet)
1 large egg
1 teaspoon water

• Preheat oven to 450°.
• Line a baking sheet with parchment paper.
• On a lightly floured surface, unroll piecrust dough. Using 2 different leaf-shaped cutters (1¾x1 inches; 2x1¼ inches), cut 6 of each shape from dough. Place dough leaves 2 inches apart on prepared baking sheet.
• Using a small, sharp knife, score leaf veins in dough leaves.
• In a small bowl, combine egg and 1 teaspoon water, whisking well to make an egg wash. Lightly brush leaves with egg wash.
• Bake until light golden brown, 5 to 6 minutes. Let cool completely.
• Store in an airtight container and serve within a day.

Roasted Butternut Squash Soup with Crispy Prosciutto

Makes approximately 8 (½-cup) servings

Sliced prosciutto, cooked until crisp, adds pleasing crunch and salty flavor to the smooth and creamy texture of this comforting soup.

6 cups cubed peeled butternut squash
1 cup chopped yellow onion
¼ cup olive oil, divided
1 teaspoon fine sea salt
1 teaspoon ground black pepper
2 cups low-sodium chicken broth, warm
½ teaspoon seasoned salt
½ teaspoon smoked paprika
1 (3-ounce) package sliced prosciutto

- Preheat oven to 400°. Line a rimmed baking sheet with foil.
- Arrange squash and onion in a single layer on prepared baking sheet. Drizzle with 2 tablespoons oil, stirring gently to coat. Sprinkle with fine sea salt and pepper.
- Bake until squash is lightly golden on edges, 20 to 24 minutes. Let cool for 5 minutes.
- In the work bowl of a food processor, pulse cooled squash mixture until roughly chopped. With processor running, slowly add broth to squash mixture, processing until smooth. Add seasoned salt and paprika, pulsing to combine.
- In a nonstick skillet, heat remaining 2 tablespoons olive oil over medium heat. Add prosciutto slices to skillet; cook until they begin to crisp, approximately 1 minute, turning each slice as needed. Drain on paper towels. Crumble over individual servings of soup. Serve immediately.

MAKE-AHEAD TIP: Soup can be made up to 3 days in advance, placed in a covered container, and refrigerated until needed. Reheat over low heat, adding more warm chicken broth to thin, if necessary.

SOUPS | *Teatime Savories* 23

- In a large saucepan, melt butter over medium-low heat. Add leeks, and cook, stirring occasionally, until tender and slightly caramelized, approximately 20 minutes. (Reduce heat if leeks start to burn.)
- Stir in broth, watercress, and pepper. Bring to a boil, then reduce heat to a simmer, and cook for 20 minutes. Remove from heat, and stir in cream.
- Using an immersion blender, purée soup until creamy and smooth.
- Garnish individual servings with a dollop of crème fraîche and a sprig of watercress, if desired.

KITCHEN TIP: *To blanch watercress, immerse it in a saucepan of boiling water for 1 minute. Remove from boiling water, and place in a bowl of ice water to stop cooking. Remove from ice water, drain well, and coarsely chop.*

Chilled Sweet Pea Soup
Makes approximately 11 (½-cup) servings

This cold soup, picture-perfect for spring and summer affairs, is equal parts refreshing and exceptional.

1 tablespoon unsalted butter
1 medium leek (white and light green portion only), chopped
3 cups reduced-sodium chicken broth
2 (10-ounce) bags frozen peas
2 tablespoons minced fresh mint leaves
2 teaspoons fine sea salt
½ cup heavy whipping cream
Garnish: fresh mint leaves

- In a large saucepan, melt butter over medium heat. Add leek, and cook, stirring occasionally, until tender, 5 to 10 minutes. Stir in broth, and bring to a boil. Stir in peas and cook until tender, 1 to 2 minutes. Stir in mint and salt. Remove from heat, and let cool slightly.
- Working in batches, transfer soup mixture to the container of a blender; blend until smooth. Transfer soup to a large bowl. Stir in cream. Let cool for 30 minutes. Cover and refrigerate overnight. Serve cold.
- Garnish individual servings with mint leaves, if desired.

Watercress Cream Soup
Makes approximately 8 (½-cup) servings

This easy-to-prepare, verdant soup combines sliced leeks, watercress, and heavy cream into a uniquely scrumptious concoction.

3 tablespoons salted butter
2 cups sliced leeks (white part only)
1 (32-ounce) carton low-sodium chicken broth
2 (4-ounce) packages watercress, blanched
⅛ teaspoon ground black pepper
2 tablespoons heavy whipping cream
Garnish: crème fraîche and 8 sprigs watercress

Wild Mushroom and Chestnut Soup
Makes approximately 12 (½-cup) servings

Laden with Vidalia onions, gourmet mushrooms, and chopped chestnuts, this vibrant soup will be the star of your next savories course.

6 tablespoons olive oil, divided
1 small Vidalia onion, finely diced
1 teaspoon garlic powder
½ teaspoon fine sea salt
½ teaspoon ground black pepper
3 (4-ounce) packages gourmet mushrooms, trimmed and divided
1 cup finely chopped chestnuts
2½ cups vegetable stock
½ cup half-and-half
½ cup heavy whipping cream
2 teaspoons lemon juice
Garnish: fresh microgreens, truffle oil, and Edible Whole-Grain Spoons (recipe follows)

- In a medium saucepan, heat 3 tablespoons oil over medium-high heat. Stir in onion, garlic powder, salt, and pepper. Cook until tender, approximately 4 minutes, stirring occasionally. Reduce heat to medium, and continue cooking for 2 minutes.
- Add 2 packages mushrooms and chestnuts, cooking for 5 minutes, stirring occasionally.
- Stir in stock. Simmer for 15 minutes.
- Stir in half-and-half, cream, and lemon juice. Cook for 5 minutes. Remove from heat, and let cool slightly.
- Meanwhile, in a small sauté pan, heat remaining 3 tablespoons oil over medium-high heat. Add remaining 1 package mushrooms, stirring to coat. Cook until tender, approximately 5 minutes, stirring occasionally. Set aside.
- Working in batches, if necessary, transfer chestnut mixture to the container of a blender. Secure lid on blender, and remove center piece of lid to let steam escape; place a clean towel over opening in lid to avoid splatters. Blend until smooth. Serve warm.
- Garnish individual servings with sautéed mushrooms, microgreens, and a drizzle of truffle oil, if desired. Serve immediately with Edible Whole-Grain Spoons.

Edible Whole-Grain Spoons
Makes 48

What could be more charming than an edible utensil to pair with your soup? These tasty accoutrements are everything that you never knew you needed for teatime.

1 large egg white
2 tablespoons sugar
¼ cup all-purpose flour
½ teaspoon fine sea salt
½ teaspoon garlic powder
1¼ tablespoons unsalted butter, melted
2 teaspoons heavy whipping cream
1 tablespoon white sesame seeds
1 tablespoon flax seeds
1 tablespoon old-fashioned oats

- In a small bowl, combine egg white and sugar. Beat at medium speed with a mixer until frothy, 1 to 2 minutes. Beat in flour, salt, and garlic powder. Beat in butter and cream until smooth, approximately 30 seconds.
- Cover batter, and refrigerate for 2 hours.
- Meanwhile, in a small bowl, stir together seeds and oats. Set aside.

- Preheat oven to 325°.
- Line a baking sheet with a silicone baking mat. Place spoon template on baking mat.*
- Using an offset spatula, spread approximately 1 tablespoon cold batter over each spoon cutout of template (Step 3). Remove plastic template (Step 4). Evenly sprinkle spoons with seed mixture (Step 5).
- Bake until lightly browned, 6 to 8 minutes. Let cool on pan for 5 minutes. Using an offset spatula, carefully remove spoons to wire racks, and let cool completely.
- Rinse plastic template, and pat dry. Repeat process with remaining batter and seed mixture.
- Serve immediately, or store spoons in an airtight container in the freezer for up to a week.

*Trace a spoon onto clear plastic or vellum the size of the baking mat (Step 1). Use an utility knife to cut out spoon shapes (Step 2).

EDITOR'S NOTE: For clarity, Steps 3 to 5 were photographed on a cutting board. However, it is best to work these steps on a baking sheet.

SOUPS | Teatime Savories 27

Shrimp Bisque
Makes 10 (½-cup) servings

A rich and creamy stock, flavored with shrimp, sweet onion, carrot, celery, herbs, and orange peel, forms the base of this delectable starter for afternoon tea.

1 pound headless medium shrimp, with shells
3 tablespoons extra-virgin olive oil
3 tablespoons salted butter
1 cup chopped sweet onion
½ cup chopped carrot
½ cup chopped celery
2 tablespoons tomato paste
¼ cup all-purpose flour
1 (32-ounce) carton seafood stock
3 sprigs fresh thyme
1 bay leaf
1 strip orange peel, approximately 6x1 inches
¾ cup heavy whipping cream
½ teaspoon fine sea salt
⅛ teaspoon ground black pepper
1 tablespoon sherry
Garnish: fresh thyme

- Peel and devein shrimp, reserving shells. Coarsely chop shrimp, cover, and refrigerate.
- In a medium stockpot, heat olive oil and butter over medium-high heat. Add onion, carrot, celery, and reserved shrimp shells. Reduce heat to medium-low. Cook, stirring occasionally, until vegetables are tender, approximately 10 minutes.
- Add tomato paste and then flour. Cook on low for 5 minutes, stirring occasionally. Add seafood stock, thyme, bay leaf, and orange peel. Bring to a boil, stirring occasionally, and reduce heat to a simmer. Cook for 45 minutes.
- Strain stock through a fine-mesh sieve, discarding solids, and return to pot. Add cream, salt, pepper, and chopped shrimp. Bring to a simmer, and cook just until shrimp turn opaque and pink, 2 to 3 minutes. Stir in sherry.
- Garnish individual servings with fresh thyme, if desired.

MAKE-AHEAD TIP: *Shrimp bisque can be made a day in advance, covered, and refrigerated. Before serving, reheat gently just until hot.*

Clam Chowder
Makes 20 (½-cup) servings

Topped with crumbled bacon, this New England favorite—made with clams, russet potatoes, yellow corn, and heavy cream—is a hearty addition to a teatime menu.

4 tablespoons salted butter
¾ cup finely chopped yellow onion
⅓ cup finely chopped celery
2 (6.5-ounce) cans clams in broth
2 (8-ounce) bottles clam broth
2 cups seafood stock
7 cups peeled, diced russet potatoes
¼ teaspoon garlic powder
¼ teaspoon ground white pepper
1 teaspoon fine sea salt
½ cup heavy whipping cream
1½ cups yellow corn kernels
Garnish: crumbled cooked bacon, minced fresh parsley

- In a large saucepan, melt butter over medium-high heat. Reduce heat to medium low, and stir in onion and celery, cooking until tender, approximately 10 minutes.
- Drain broth from clams (reserving clams), and add broth to cooked vegetables.
- Add bottled clam broth, seafood stock, potatoes, garlic powder, white pepper, and salt. Bring to a boil, and then reduce heat to a simmer. Cook until potatoes are very tender, approximately 15 minutes. Stir in cream.
- Using a handheld immersion blender in a deep bowl or a regular blender, purée 2 cups soup. Return purée to pot, stirring until combined. Add corn and reserved clams, and heat through.
- Garnish individual servings with bacon and parsley, if desired.

QUICHE
LORRAINE
page 40

SCRUMPTIOUS

Quiches & Pastries

FOR CELEBRATORY GATHERINGS OR
TEA LUNCHEONS, THESE TRIED-AND-TRUE DELIGHTS
ARE PROVEN TO BE EXCELLENT.

Mushroom-Leek Quiche Squares
Makes 16

Offer guests a gluten-free savory option of fluffy, crustless quiche that is studded with sharp Cheddar cheese, mushrooms, and leeks.

2 tablespoons unsalted butter, divided
8 ounces white button mushrooms, sliced
1 cup chopped leeks (white part only)
6 large eggs
2 cups heavy whipping cream
1 teaspoon chopped fresh thyme
½ teaspoon fine sea salt
¼ teaspoon ground black pepper
2 cups coarsely shredded sharp Cheddar cheese
Garnish: baby arugula and chopped tiny tomatoes

• Preheat oven to 350°. Spray a 9-inch square baking pan with cooking spray.
• In a small sauté pan, melt 1 tablespoon butter over medium-low heat. Add mushrooms, and cover pan. Cook, stirring occasionally, until mushrooms are tender, 5 to 7 minutes. Drain mushrooms well. Place in a small bowl; set aside.
• In another sauté pan, melt remaining 1 tablespoon butter over medium-low heat. Add leeks, and cover pan. Cook over low heat, stirring occasionally, until leeks are very tender, approximately 10 minutes.
• In a medium bowl, whisk together eggs, cream, thyme, salt, and pepper until well combined.
• In bottom of prepared baking pan, evenly layer 1 cup cheese, half of cooked mushrooms, and half of cooked leeks. Repeat layers.
• Whisk egg mixture again and gently pour mixture over cheese and vegetables.
• Bake until quiche edges are golden brown and center is set, 40 to 43 minutes. (Mixture will puff up and then fall as it cools.) Let quiche cool to room temperature.
• Using a sharp knife, cut and discard rough edges from quiche. Cut quiche into 16 squares.
• Just before serving, garnish with baby arugula and tiny tomatoes, if desired.

MAKE-AHEAD TIP: Make quiche and let come to room temperature up to 2 hours before serving. Quiche can also be made a day in advance, covered, and refrigerated until needed. Serve warm, at room temperature, or cold, according to preference. Garnish just before serving.

Caramelized Leek & Pancetta Quiche
Makes 1 (8-inch)

Offer guests irresistible slices of quiche laced with notes of caramelized leeks, nutty Gruyère cheese, and salty, crispy pancetta.

½ (14.1-ounce) package refrigerated piecrust dough (1 sheet)
1 tablespoon unsalted butter
1 cup thinly sliced leeks, white part only
¾ cup shredded Gruyère cheese
⅓ cup chopped crisp-cooked thinly sliced pancetta
¾ cup heavy whipping cream
2 large eggs
1 teaspoon chopped fresh thyme
¼ teaspoon fine sea salt
¼ teaspoon ground black pepper

- Preheat oven to 450°. Lightly spray an 8-inch removable-bottom, fluted tart pan with cooking spray.
- Press piecrust dough into bottom and up sides of prepared tart pan. Using the wide end of a chopstick, gently press dough into indentations in sides of pan. Trim excess dough. Using a fork, prick bottom of dough. Place a sheet of foil large enough to cover bottom of crust in pan, and weigh down with pie weights or dried beans.
- Bake for 8 to 10 minutes. Remove weights and foil. Bake until crust is golden brown, 8 to 10 minutes more. Let cool completely in pan.
- Reduce oven to 350°.
- Place cooled tartlet pan with crust on a rimmed baking sheet.
- In a small sauté pan, melt butter over medium-high heat. Stir in leeks until coated with butter. Reduce heat to medium-low, and cook, stirring frequently, until leeks are tender and starting to caramelize, 8 to 10 minutes. (Reduce heat to low if leeks are browning too much.) Let cool. Coarsely chop leeks.
- Into cooled crust, layer cheese, leeks, and pancetta, scattering each layer evenly.
- In a large liquid-measuring cup, whisk together cream, eggs, thyme, salt, and pepper until well combined. Pour into prepared crust.
- Bake quiche until set and slightly puffed, 23 to 25 minutes. Let cool to room temperature before cutting. Serve quiche within 4 hours.

MAKE-AHEAD TIP: *Quiche can be made a day in advance, wrapped well, and refrigerated. Just before serving, cut quiche into pieces, place on a parchment-lined rimmed baking sheet, and warm in a 350° oven for 5 to 8 minutes.*

Mini Zucchini Quiches
Makes 8

Baby Swiss cheese and diced zucchini star in these individually portioned quiches. To prevent excess moisture in the quiches, be sure to use primarily the outer green portions of the zucchini.

2 (14.1-ounce) packages refrigerated piecrust dough (4 sheets)
1 teaspoon olive oil
1 cup diced zucchini (approximately 1 medium zucchini)
½ teaspoon fine sea salt, divided
¼ teaspoon ground black pepper, divided
2 tablespoons thinly sliced chives
2 large eggs
⅔ cup heavy whipping cream
1 ounce (approximately ¼ cup) finely shredded baby Swiss cheese

- Preheat oven to 450°. Lightly spray 8 (4x2-inch) fluted tartlet pans with cooking spray.
- On a lightly floured surface, unroll pie dough sheets. Cut 2 (6x4-inch) rectangles from each sheet of dough. Transfer each rectangle to a prepared tartlet pan, pressing into bottoms and up sides. Using the wide end of a chopstick, gently press dough into indentations in sides of pans. Using a rolling pin or fingers, trim excess dough. Using a fork, prick bottom of dough in each tartlet pan. Place tartlet pans on a rimmed baking sheet. Freeze for 10 minutes.
- Bake until edges of tartlet shells are lightly golden brown, approximately 10 minutes. Let cool completely in pans on a wire rack.
- Reduce heat to 375°. Arrange oven rack in lower third of oven.
- In a small skillet, heat oil over medium-high heat. Add zucchini, ¼ teaspoon salt, and ⅛ teaspoon pepper. Cook, stirring frequently, until zucchini is lightly browned and just soft, 3 to 4 minutes. Let cool. Stir in chives.
- In the container of a blender, pulse together eggs, cream, remaining ¼ teaspoon salt, and remaining ⅛ teaspoon pepper until smooth and slightly foamy. Transfer mixture to a liquid-measuring cup with a pouring spout or a small bowl.
- Divide cheese evenly among prepared shells. Top cheese in each shell with 1 tablespoon zucchini mixture. Top zucchini mixture with 3 tablespoons egg mixture in each shell.
- Bake until filling is slightly puffed, approximately 15 to 16 minutes. Let cool in pans for 5 minutes before carefully removing. Serve warm or at room temperature.

MAKE-AHEAD TIP: Quiches can be made a day in advance and stored in a covered container in the refrigerator. Reheat on a rimmed baking sheet in a 350° oven until warm, approximately 5 minutes. Serve immediately.

Black Forest Ham Quiches
Makes 16

Yellow cherry tomatoes top each flavorful quiche to create the crown of this perfect bite that is constructed to resemble an upturned-brim hat.

1 (14.1-ounce) package refrigerated piecrust dough (2 sheets)
¼ cup finely chopped Black Forest ham
½ cup heavy whipping cream
1 large egg, room temperature
¼ teaspoon fine sea salt
⅛ teaspoon ground black pepper
⅛ teaspoon finely chopped fresh thyme
Garnish: 8 yellow cherry tomatoes, halved, and fresh thyme sprigs

- Preheat oven to 450°. Lightly spray 16 (2-inch) round fluted tartlet pans with cooking spray.
- On a lightly floured surface, unroll piecrust dough sheets. Using a 3-inch round cutter, cut 8 rounds from each sheet. Transfer each round to a prepared tartlet pan, pressing into bottom and up sides. Using the wide end of a chopstick, gently press dough into indentations in sides of pans. Trim excess dough. Place tartlet pans on a rimmed baking sheet. Refrigerate for 15 minutes.
- Place a small piece of parchment paper or a mini baking cup in center of each prepared tartlet pan, letting ends extend over edges of pan, and fill with ceramic pie weights or dried beans.
- Bake for 8 minutes. Carefully remove pie weights and parchment paper. Bake for 5 minutes more. Let cool completely in pans on a wire rack.
- Reduce oven temperature to 350°.
- Divide ham among cooled tartlet shells.
- In a medium bowl, whisk together cream, egg, salt, pepper, and thyme. Pour evenly over ham in tartlet shells.
- Bake until centers of quiches are set, 12 to 14 minutes. Let cool slightly on a wire rack before carefully removing quiches from pans.
- Garnish each quiche with a tomato half and thyme sprigs, if desired. Serve immediately.

MAKE-AHEAD TIP: Quiches can be made a day in advance and stored in a covered container in the refrigerator. Reheat on a rimmed baking sheet in a 350° oven until warm, approximately 5 minutes. Garnish just before serving.

- In a large liquid-measuring cup, whisk together eggs, cream, salt, and pepper. Divide egg mixture evenly among wells of prepared pan, filling to just below rims.
- Bake until eggs are set and frittatas are slightly puffed, 8 to 10 minutes. Let frittatas cool to room temperature before removing from pan.
- Top each frittata with a dollop of crème fraîche.
- Cut remaining 4 ounces salmon into 24 evenly sized pieces. Shape each piece into a cone, and place atop crème fraîche, seam side down.
- Garnish each frittata with a dill sprig, if desired. Serve immediately.

*We used a Chicago Metallic nonstick 24-well mini muffin pan, available at cmbakeware.com.

MAKE-AHEAD TIP: *Frittatas can be made earlier in the day, placed in a covered container, and refrigerated. Let come to room temperature before topping and serving.*

Mini Smoked Salmon, Gruyère & Herb Frittatas
Makes 24

Notes of dill and chive—with a dollop of crème fraîche and a smoked salmon rosette—give these eye-catching servings vivacious flavor.

2 (4-ounce) packages thinly sliced smoked salmon, divided
½ cup finely shredded Gruyère cheese
¼ cup finely chopped fresh dill
¼ cup finely chopped fresh chives
7 large eggs
2 tablespoons heavy whipping cream
¼ teaspoon fine sea salt
⅛ teaspoon ground black pepper
1 (8-ounce) container crème fraîche
Garnish: fresh dill sprigs

- Preheat oven to 350°.
- Spray a shallow 24-well mini muffin pan* with cooking spray.
- Finely chop 4 ounces salmon. Divide salmon evenly among wells of prepared pan. Top salmon evenly with cheese and herbs.

Asparagus-Pancetta Quiche
Makes 1 (9-inch) quiche (approximately 8 servings)

Creamy Havarti cheese, crispy pancetta, and roasted fresh asparagus form a delicious flavor trio in this satisfying quiche.

½ (14.1-ounce) package refrigerated piecrust dough (1 sheet)
½ bunch thin fresh asparagus
¼ teaspoon extra-virgin olive oil
⅜ teaspoon fine sea salt, divided
¼ teaspoon ground black pepper, divided
½ cup heavy whipping cream
2 large eggs
½ teaspoon chopped fresh thyme leaves
⅓ cup finely shredded Havarti cheese
⅓ cup chopped cooked pancetta

- Preheat oven to 450°.
- On a lightly floured surface, unroll piecrust dough. Transfer dough to a 9-inch removable-bottom, fluted tart pan, pressing dough into bottom of pan. Using a finger or the wide end of a chopstick, press dough into indentations in sides of pan. Trim excess dough. Refrigerate for 30 minutes.

- Using a fork, prick dough all over in bottom of pan.
- Bake until tart shell is light golden brown, 7 to 9 minutes. Let cool completely on a wire rack.
- Reduce oven temperature to 400°.
- Snap and discard tough ends from asparagus. Lay asparagus spears in a single layer on a rimmed baking sheet. Drizzle asparagus with olive oil and sprinkle with ⅛ teaspoon salt and ⅛ teaspoon pepper.
- Roast until asparagus feels tender when pierced with the tip of a sharp knife, approximately 7 minutes. Transfer roasted asparagus spears to a clean surface. Using a sharp knife, chop asparagus into bite-size pieces.
- Reduce oven temperature to 350°.
- In a liquid-measuring cup, whisk together cream, eggs, thyme, remaining ¼ teaspoon salt, and remaining ⅛ teaspoon pepper until thoroughly combined.
- Sprinkle cheese evenly into bottom of cooled tart shell. Scatter asparagus and pancetta over cheese. Pour cream mixture into shell, filling just below top edge.
- Bake until quiche is slightly puffed and lightly browned, 19 to 21 minutes. Let cool for 15 minutes before cutting and serving.

MAKE-AHEAD TIP: Quiche can be baked a day in advance and stored in a covered container in the refrigerator. Reheat on a rimmed baking sheet in a 350° oven for 6 to 8 minutes.

Petite Ham & Cheese Quiches
Makes 17

The cherished flavor combination of ham and cheese is on display in these tiny quiches.

1 (14.1-ounce) package refrigerated piecrust dough (2 sheets)
½ cup finely grated Jarlsberg cheese
½ cup heavy whipping cream
1 large egg
½ teaspoon finely chopped fresh chives
¼ teaspoon fine sea salt
⅛ teaspoon ground black pepper
¼ cup finely chopped ham

- Preheat oven to 450°. Lightly spray 17 (2-inch) round fluted tartlet pans with cooking spray. Line bottoms of pans with parchment paper rounds.
- On a lightly floured surface, unroll piecrust dough sheets. Using a 2½-inch round cutter, cut 17 rounds from dough. Transfer each dough round to a prepared tartlet pan, pressing into bottom and up sides. Using the wide end of a chopstick, gently press dough into indentations in sides of pans. Trim excess dough. Place tartlet pans on a rimmed baking sheet. Refrigerate for 30 minutes. (This will help prevent shrinkage during baking.)
- Prick bottoms of tartlet shells with a fork to prevent puffing while baking.
- Bake tartlet shells until light golden brown, approximately 7 minutes. Let cool completely. Reduce oven temperature to 350°.
- Divide cheese evenly among tartlet shells.
- In a large measuring cup with a pouring spout, whisk together cream, egg, chives, salt, and pepper until blended. Divide mixture evenly among tartlet shells. Sprinkle evenly with ham.
- Bake until centers of quiches are set, approximately 14 minutes. Let cool in pans for 10 minutes. Carefully remove quiches from pans. Serve warm or at room temperature within 2 hours.

MAKE-AHEAD TIP: Quiches can be baked a day in advance and stored in a covered container in the refrigerator. Reheat on a rimmed baking sheet in a 350° oven for 6 to 8 minutes before serving.

Lamb Puff Pastry Roulades
Makes 32 slices

A flaky exterior encases a delicious filling of free-range lamb, carrots, cheeses, and green peas in one mouthwatering pastry. An apple jelly glaze adds unexpected complementary sweetness and lovely shine.

2 tablespoons extra-virgin olive oil
1 pound ground free-range lamb
1½ teaspoons herbes de Provence
½ teaspoon garlic salt
¼ teaspoon ground black pepper
¼ cup coarsely chopped matchstick carrots
1 (17.3-ounce) package puff pastry (2 sheets), slightly thawed
¼ cup whole-grain French mustard*
¼ cup yellow mustard
1 cup shredded Gruyère cheese
½ cup freshly grated Parmesan cheese
¼ cup frozen baby green peas, thawed
2 tablespoons finely chopped fresh parsley
1 large egg
1 tablespoon water
Garnish: melted apple jelly

- Preheat oven to 400°. Line 2 rimmed baking sheets with parchment paper.
- In a medium sauté pan, heat oil over medium-high heat until shimmering. Add lamb, stirring and breaking apart with a spoon. Add herbes de Provence, garlic salt, and pepper. Cook, stirring occasionally, until meat is browned and no longer pink. During last minute of cooking, add carrots. Drain meat mixture well in a paper towel–lined bowl.
- Using a rolling pin, roll out puff pastry sheets to 13x9-inch rectangles.
- In a small bowl, stir together mustards until combined. Spread over puff pastry sheets, leaving a 1-inch border around all sides.
- Scatter lamb mixture over mustard layer. Sprinkle cheeses over lamb. Scatter peas and parsley over cheeses, pressing into puff pastry gently with palm of hand to adhere.
- Starting at one long end of each puff pastry sheet, roll up, firmly encasing ingredients, pinching edge to seal, and ending with seam side down. Press and tuck ends under.

- Using a serrated knife, trim and discard ends of roulades. Cut each roulade into 16 even slices. Place slices, cut side down, onto prepared baking sheets.
- In a small bowl, whisk together egg and 1 tablespoon water to make an egg wash. Brush tops of roulade slices with egg wash.
- Bake until edges of roulade slices are light golden brown, 15 to 18 minutes.
- Just before serving, brush slices with melted jelly, if desired.

*We used Maille Old Style Mustard.

MAKE-AHEAD TIP: *Up to a day in advance, assemble roulades, wrap in plastic wrap, and refrigerate until ready to bake.*

Quiche Lorraine
Makes 1 (9-inch) quiche

Topped with a delectable, fresh Arugula Salad, this classic quiche—flavored by chopped bacon and ground nutmeg—is sure to satisfy.

½ (14.1-ounce) package refrigerated piecrust dough (1 sheet)
1 large egg white, lightly beaten
⅓ cup chopped cooked bacon
3 large eggs
1 cup heavy whipping cream
½ teaspoon fine sea salt
⅛ teaspoon ground black pepper
⅛ teaspoon ground nutmeg
Garnish: Arugula Salad (recipe follows) and additional ground black pepper

• Preheat oven to 450°. Lightly spray a 9-inch removable-bottom, fluted tart pan with cooking spray.
• Place piecrust dough in prepared tart pan. Using the large end of a chopstick, press dough into indentations in sides of pan. Trim and discard excess dough. Using a fork, prick bottom of dough. Place tart pan on a rimmed baking sheet, and freeze for 15 minutes.
• Bake until tart shell is lightly golden brown, approximately 7 minutes. Let cool completely.
• Brush egg white onto bottom of tart shell. Bake until egg white is set and looks shiny, approximately 3 minutes. (This will help seal tart shell and prevent sogginess). Let cool completely.
• Reduce oven temperature to 350°. Scatter bacon pieces in cooled tart shell.
• In a medium bowl, whisk together eggs, cream, salt, pepper, and nutmeg until combined. Pour mixture over bacon.
• Bake quiche until filling is set, approximately 25 minutes. Let cool to room temperature.
• Garnish with Arugula Salad and a sprinkle of black pepper, if desired.

Arugula Salad
Makes 1 cup

Baby arugula, tiny tomatoes, and olive oil combine to create this simple, yet oh-so tasty, salad. Use it as a quiche topping, as pictured on opposite page, or enjoy it alone.

1 cup fresh baby arugula
¼ cup halved cherry and grape tomatoes
½ teaspoon extra-virgin olive oil

• In a small bowl, toss together arugula, tomatoes, and oil. Serve immediately.

Roast Pork Salad Mini Phyllo Cups
Makes 24

Pork tenderloin, white button mushrooms, fresh thyme, and Worcestershire sauce combine to create a sumptuous filling to be presented in petite phyllo cups.

1 pound pork tenderloin
1 tablespoon plus 1 teaspoon olive oil, divided
⅛ teaspoon garlic salt
⅛ teaspoon ground black pepper
2 cups sliced white button mushrooms
1 teaspoon fresh thyme leaves
⅛ teaspoon fine sea salt
¼ cup mayonnaise
2 tablespoons stone-ground mustard
¼ teaspoon Worcestershire sauce
24 frozen mini phyllo cups*, thawed
Garnish: fresh thyme sprigs

• Preheat oven to 350°.
• Line a rimmed baking sheet with foil. Place pork tenderloin on prepared baking sheet, drizzle with 1 teaspoon oil, and season with garlic salt and pepper.
• Roast until a meat thermometer inserted in the thickest part of tenderloin registers 145°, approximately 25 minutes. (Pork will be pink inside; cook longer for well done.) Let stand for 15 minutes.
• Using a sharp knife, cut tenderloin into ½-inch slices. Cut each slice lengthwise into ¼-inch pieces, and then cut crosswise into ¼-inch cubes.
• Line another rimmed baking sheet with parchment paper.

• In a medium bowl, toss mushrooms with remaining 1 tablespoon oil, thyme, and salt. Spread in a single layer on prepared baking sheet.
• Roast until mushrooms are tender and release their juices, approximately 20 minutes. Let cool completely. Chop mushrooms very finely.
• In a medium bowl, combine chopped pork, chopped mushrooms, mayonnaise, mustard, and Worcestershire sauce, stirring to blend. Fill each phyllo cup with pork salad.
• Garnish each phyllo cup with a thyme sprig, if desired. Serve immediately.

*We used Athens Phyllo Shells.

MAKE-AHEAD TIP: *Pork salad can be made a day in advance, covered, and refrigerated until needed.*

Asparagus-Topped Frittata Bites
Makes 16

These wonderfully springy bites, crowned with asparagus and crème fraîche, grace our cover. Hashbrown potatoes, Parmesan cheese, and fresh herbs mingle terrifically with egg in this frittata.

2 tablespoons olive oil
2 cups refrigerated hash brown potatoes
2 cloves garlic, minced
1¼ teaspoons fine sea salt, divided
½ teaspoon ground black pepper, divided
12 large eggs
¾ cup freshly grated Parmesan cheese (approximately 2.5 ounces)
¼ cup plus 2 tablespoons heavy whipping cream
¼ cup chopped fresh parsley
3 tablespoons chopped fresh chives
1 tablespoon fresh chervil or 1 teaspoon dried chervil
16 spears fresh asparagus
⅔ cup crème fraîche

- Preheat oven to 350°. Spray bottom and sides of an 8-inch square baking pan with cooking spray.
- In a large skillet, heat oil over medium heat. Add potatoes, and cook, stirring occasionally, for 3 minutes. Add garlic, ¼ teaspoon salt, and ¼ teaspoon pepper, and cook, stirring occasionally, until potatoes are tender, 1 to 2 minutes. Transfer to prepared baking pan. Using an offset spatula, spread potatoes in an even layer.
- In a large bowl, whisk together eggs, cheese, cream, parsley, chives, chervil, remaining 1 teaspoon salt, and remaining ¼ teaspoon pepper until well blended. Pour egg mixture over potatoes.
- Bake until eggs are set, 25 to 30 minutes. Let cool on a wire rack for 30 minutes. Cover and refrigerate until cold, at least 2 hours or overnight.
- Using a sharp knife, cut 1½ inches off the tip end of each asparagus spear. (Reserve stem ends for another use, if desired.)
- In a small saucepan of boiling salted water, cook asparagus tips just until bright green and crisp-tender, 1 to 2 minutes. Remove with a slotted spoon and immediately drop into ice water. Drain, and pat dry.
- Using a sharp knife, trim and discard ½ inch from edges of frittata; cut frittata into 16 squares.
- Place crème fraîche in a piping bag fitted with a drop flower tip (Wilton #2D). Pipe crème fraîche rosettes onto each frittata square. Top each with an asparagus tip. Serve immediately.

Springtime Vegetable Tartlets
Makes 12

Colorful asparagus, radishes, and peas rest atop a tangy goat cheese filling in these charming tartlets.

12 spears fresh asparagus
1 (14.1-ounce) package refrigerated piecrust dough (2 sheets)
1 (4-ounce) package goat cheese
2 tablespoons whole yogurt
⅛ teaspoon smoked paprika
⅛ teaspoon ground white pepper
1 tablespoon fresh lemon juice
1 teaspoon fresh thyme leaves
3 tablespoons olive oil
2 medium radishes, thinly sliced and cut into half circles
¼ cup fresh or frozen English peas

42 *Teatime Savories* | QUICHES & PASTRIES

- Using a sharp knife, cut 2 inches off the tip end of each asparagus spear. (Reserve stem ends for another use, if desired.)
- In a small saucepan of boiling salted water, cook asparagus tips just until bright green and crisp, 1 to 2 minutes. Remove with a slotted spoon and immediately drop into ice water. Drain, and pat dry. Using a sharp knife, cut each tip in half lengthwise.
- Preheat oven to 425°. Spray 12 (2-inch) fluted tartlet pans with baking spray with flour.
- On a lightly floured surface, unroll dough. Using a rolling pin, roll out dough to a ⅛-inch thickness. Using a 3-inch round cutter dipped in flour, cut 12 rounds from dough. Transfer each dough round to a prepared tartlet pan, pressing into bottom and up sides. Using the wide end of a chopstick, gently press dough into indentations in sides of pans. Trim excess dough. Place tartlet pans on a rimmed baking sheet.
- Top each tartlet pan with a small parchment paper square or a paper cupcake liner, letting ends extend over edges, and fill with ceramic pie weights or dried beans.
- Bake until tartlet shell edges are lightly golden, approximately 8 minutes. Let cool for 5 minutes before carefully removing weights and parchment. Let cool completely before carefully removing tartlet shells from pans.
- In a small bowl, stir together goat cheese, yogurt, paprika, and pepper. Transfer goat cheese mixture to a piping bag fitted with a large round tip. Pipe mixture into each tartlet shell.
- In a medium bowl, stir together lemon juice and thyme. Gradually add oil, whisking constantly, until fully incorporated. Add asparagus, radishes, and peas, tossing to coat. Arrange 2 asparagus pieces, 3 radish half circles, and 4 English peas in each tartlet. Serve immediately.

MAKE-AHEAD TIP: Tartlet shells can be prepared early in the day, cooled completely, and stored in an airtight container. Goat cheese filling can be prepared up to a day in advance, covered, and refrigerated. Stir well before using.

Heirloom Tomato Tart
Makes 8 servings

A flaky pastry crust holds layers of colorful heirloom tomato slices and a luscious, cheesy filling.

4 to 5 heirloom tomatoes (various colors and sizes)
½ teaspoon fine sea salt
½ (14.1-ounce) package refrigerated piecrust dough (1 sheet)
1½ cups coarsely grated, sharp yellow Cheddar cheese
½ cup mayonnaise
2 tablespoons chopped fresh flat-leaf parsley
1 tablespoon chopped green onion
¼ teaspoon ground black pepper
1 tablespoon red wine vinegar
1 teaspoon olive oil
Garnish: additional ground black pepper and additional chopped fresh parsley

- Preheat oven to 350°.
- With a sharp knife, slice tomatoes, cutting larger tomatoes into ¼-inch slices for bottom layer and smaller tomatoes into ⅛-inch slices for top layer. Arrange tomato slices in a single layer on paper towels, and sprinkle with salt. Let stand for 30 minutes.
- Unroll piecrust dough, and press into a 9-inch removable-bottom, fluted tart pan, trimming and discarding excess dough.
- In a medium bowl, stir together cheese, mayonnaise, parsley, green onion, and pepper. Using an offset spatula, spread half of cheese mixture into bottom of tart pan in a thin even layer.
- Blot tomatoes dry with additional paper towels. Place a large tomato slice in center of pan on top of cheese mixture. Cut several large tomato slices in half, and arrange around center tomato slice. Cut remaining large slices into quarters to fill in spaces between tomato slices, creating a base layer.
- Spread remaining cheese mixture in an even layer on top of tomatoes.
- Arrange thinner tomato slices on top of cheese layer in a pleasing pattern. Sprinkle with vinegar, and drizzle with olive oil.
- Bake until crust is deep golden brown and cheese mixture is hot and beginning to bubble, 25 to 30 minutes. Remove from oven, and let cool slightly before removing from tart pan.
- Just before serving, garnish with pepper and parsley, if desired. Serve at room temperature within 3 hours.

Chicken Cordon Bleu Pastry Swirls
Makes 10

Flaky puff pastry encases layers of deli-style chicken and ham slices along with Gruyère and Parmesan cheeses for a savory teatime treat that mimics the traditional flavors of the iconic entrée. Pictured with Champagne & Tarragon Radish Flower Canapés (page 107) and Pastrami-Avocado Tea Sandwiches (page 83).

½ (17.3-ounce) package frozen puff pastry (1 sheet), slightly thawed
2 tablespoons coarse-ground country-style Dijon mustard
4 slices deli-style roast chicken
2 slices deli-style smoked ham
¾ cup coarsely shredded Gruyère cheese*
¼ cup finely grated Parmesan cheese*
1 teaspoon chopped fresh thyme
⅛ teaspoon ground black pepper
1 large egg
1 tablespoon water
Garnish: fresh thyme sprigs

- Preheat oven to 400°. Line a rimmed baking sheet with parchment paper.
- On a lightly floured surface and using a rolling pin, roll out puff pastry sheet to a ⅛-inch thickness (approximately 12x10-inches).
- Spread mustard evenly on puff pastry to within 1 inch of edges. Top mustard layer evenly with chicken slices and then ham slices. Scatter cheeses evenly over ham. Sprinkle thyme and pepper evenly over cheeses.
- In a small bowl, whisk together egg and 1 tablespoon water to make an egg wash. Brush a thin layer of egg wash onto pastry border of a long side of puff pastry.
- Starting at the other long side, roll up pastry firmly and evenly to encase ingredients and form a cylinder. Pinch long edge into a seam and turn pastry roll so that seam side is down. Pinch ends together and tuck under. Refrigerate pastry roll for 30 minutes.
- Using a thin-bladed serrated bread knife in a gentle sawing motion, cut ends from pastry roll and discard ends. Cut roll into 10 (approximately 1-inch) slices. Lay slices on prepared baking sheet. Brush pastry slices with remaining egg mixture.
- Bake until golden brown, 15 to 17 minutes.
- Garnish with fresh thyme sprigs, if desired. Serve warm.

*Because pre-grated and pre-shredded cheeses have additives that can impact their texture, we recommend grating or shredding cheese from a block just before using.

MAKE-AHEAD TIP: Pastry roll can be assembled up to a day in advance, wrapped in plastic wrap, and refrigerated. Slice and bake just before serving.

KITCHEN TIP: Use a bench scraper to help with rolling up pastry.

Savory Gruyère Palmiers
Makes 10

Puff pastry spread with Dijon mustard covers nutty Gruyère cheese in these rich palmiers baked in heart shapes.

½ (17.3-ounce) package frozen puff pastry (1 sheet), slightly thawed
2 tablespoons coarse-grain Dijon mustard
½ cup shredded Gruyère cheese
½ teaspoon chopped fresh thyme
⅛ teaspoon ground black pepper
1 large egg
1 tablespoon water

• Preheat oven to 400°. Line a rimmed baking sheet with parchment paper.
• Using a rolling pin, roll out puff pastry sheet on a lightly floured surface into a 10-inch square. (Puff pastry should be thawed but still firm.)
• Spread mustard in an even layer onto puff pastry, leaving a 1-inch border around edges. Sprinkle evenly with cheese, thyme, and pepper.
• Mark dough at top and bottom edges at the halfway point. Fold in opposite sides of the dough square (right and left edges) so the sides are halfway from the center (a ¼ fold). Using a rolling pin, lightly roll dough to laminate. Fold opposite sides again toward center, meeting at the marked halfway point of dough square. Lightly roll dough again to laminate. Fold right half of dough lengthwise over left half of dough. Using a rolling pin, roll dough again lightly to laminate. (This will keep pastries from puffing up too much.)
• Using a sharp knife, trim and discard ends of dough stack. Cut folded dough into 10 (approximately 1-inch-wide) slices. Place slices, cut sides down, onto prepared baking sheet. Pinch bottom fold of each slice into a point. (Tops of pastries should be slightly separated—this will create a heart shape when baked.)
• In a small bowl, whisk together egg and 1 tablespoon water to make an egg wash. Brush tops of palmier slices with egg wash.
• Bake until pastries are lightly golden brown, 14 to 16 minutes. Serve warm.

Beef-Mushroom Carbonnade in Pastry Shells
Makes 8

Braised beef and chocolate might seem like an unusual combination in this savory creation. But take our word for it, this hearty bite is beautifully balanced and remarkably tasty thanks to a filling of tender beef, chopped vegetables, and a hint of bittersweet chocolate all housed inside a buttery pastry shell.

2 tablespoons extra-virgin olive oil
1 pound beef stew meat
¼ teaspoon garlic salt
⅛ teaspoon ground black pepper
½ cup chopped yellow onion
2 cups chopped baby bella mushrooms
2 teaspoons minced garlic
1 tablespoon tomato paste
2 slices stale rye bread
1 cup very hot water
1 teaspoon beef bouillon paste
½ cup small-diced carrots
1 bay leaf
½ teaspoon dried thyme
½ cup dry red wine
2 tablespoons finely chopped bittersweet chocolate
2 (10-ounce) packages frozen puff pastry shells
1 large egg
1 tablespoon water
Garnish: chopped fresh parsley

46 | Teatime Savories | QUICHES & PASTRIES

- Preheat oven to 275°.
- Heat oil in a heavy braising pot or a Dutch oven* over medium-high heat. Cut meat into 1-inch cubes. Season with garlic salt and pepper. Brown meat in batches so it is not overcrowded. Cook, turning meat and browning well on both sides. (If meat is browning too quickly, reduce heat. Add a little more oil, if needed, while browning.) Remove meat with a slotted spoon. Cut meat pieces in half to further reduce their size so meat will fit nicely inside pastry shells.
- Add onions to drippings in pot; cook over medium-low heat, stirring frequently until golden brown, 5 to 7 minutes, and adding a little more oil, if needed. Stir in mushrooms and garlic; cook until mushrooms begin to release their juices. Stir in tomato paste.
- In the work bowl of a food processor, pulse bread until fine crumbs form.
- In a small bowl, stir together 1 cup hot water and bouillon paste until bouillon dissolves.
- To mushroom mixture in pot, add breadcrumbs, carrots, bay leaf, thyme, red wine, and bouillon mixture, stirring to loosen browned bits from bottom of pot. Bring to a boil. Return meat to pot. Cover pot with lid and place in oven.
- Braise until beef is very tender, approximately 2 hours, stirring and checking a few times during cooking time to make sure liquid is not cooking out. Remove and discard bay leaf. Stir in chocolate until melted. (Mixture should be a creamy gravy. If mixture seems too thick, add extra beef broth.) Keep warm.
- Increase oven temperature to 425°. Line a rimmed baking sheet with parchment paper.
- Place frozen puff pastry shells, evenly spaced, on prepared baking sheet.
- In a small bowl, whisk together egg and 1 tablespoon water to make an egg wash. Brush tops of frozen shells with egg wash, making sure mixture does not run down sides.
- Bake until shells are puffed and golden brown, 18 to 20 minutes. Let cool slightly. Remove center of tops and inner layers from shells. Fill shells with warm meat mixture.
- Garnish with parsley, if desired. Serve immediately.

*Braise meat mixture in a pot with a heavy lid. If lid does not fit tightly, cover pan with a sheet of foil under lid to keep steam from escaping while braising in oven.

MAKE-AHEAD TIP: Meat mixture can be made a day in advance and stored in a covered container in the refrigerator. Reheat gently over low heat. If too thick, add a little extra beef bouillon mixture.

Roast Beef Pastries
Makes 12

Strips of puff pastry are layered with a luscious aïoli, mozzarella cheese, and roast beef before being folded accordion style, placed in a muffin pan, and baked. They are pictured with Loaded Potato Twists (page 121).

¼ cup mayonnaise
2 tablespoons sour cream
1 tablespoon prepared horseradish
½ teaspoon Worcestershire sauce
½ teaspoon honey
1 (17.3-ounce) package frozen puff pastry, thawed (2 sheets)
⅓ cup shredded mozzarella cheese
6 ultra-thin slices deli-style roast beef*

- Preheat oven to 400°. Spray a 12-well muffin pan with cooking spray.
- In a small bowl, whisk together mayonnaise, sour cream, horseradish, Worcestershire sauce, and honey to make an aïoli. Refrigerate until ready to use.
- On a lightly floured surface using a rolling pin and working with one puff pastry sheet at a time, roll puff pastry into a 12-inch square (approximately ⅛-inch thick). Using a pizza wheel or a thin, sharp knife, cut each dough square into 6 (12x2-inch) strips. Using a small offset spatula, spread a scant 1 tablespoon aïoli in a thin even layer onto each dough strip, leaving an approximately ½-inch border on all sides. Sprinkle cheese over aïoli layer, approximately ½ tablespoon per strip. Cut roast beef slices in half, and place a piece in the center of each dough strip. Working with a strip at a time, fold pastry back and forth onto itself 3 times, accordion style. Place each folded pastry into a well of prepared muffin pan with meat facing up.
- Bake for 15 minutes. Reduce oven temperature to 350° and continue baking until tops and sides are evenly golden brown, 10 to 15 minutes more. Let cool slightly in pan, 5 to 6 minutes. Serve warm.

*If roast beef slices are small, additional slices may be needed.

Reuben Swirls
Makes 12

Inspired by the traditional deli sandwich, these puff-pastry swirls reimagine the ingredients of the lunch favorite (corned beef, Swiss cheese, sauerkraut, and Russian dressing) into a three-bite morsel apropos for afternoon tea.

½ (17.3-ounce) package frozen puff pastry (1 sheet), slightly thawed
Russian Dressing (recipe follows)
4 large thin slices corned beef
4 large thin slices Swiss cheese
½ cup well-drained sauerkraut
1 large egg
1 tablespoon water

- Preheat oven to 400°. Line a rimmed baking sheet with parchment paper.
- Place puff pastry sheet on a lightly floured surface. Using a rolling pin, roll out pastry sheet slightly to flatten and make pliable.
- Spread 2 tablespoons Russian Dressing onto puff pastry, leaving a 1-inch border around edge. Top with corned beef slices and cheese within 1-inch border. Sprinkle sauerkraut evenly over cheese. Starting at a short end, roll up pastry firmly and evenly to form a cylinder and encase ingredients. Using a serrated knife, cut into ½-inch slices. Place slices, evenly spaced, on prepared baking sheet.
- In a small bowl, whisk together egg and water to create an egg wash. Brush egg wash over tops of pastries.
- Bake until pastries are light golden brown, 13 to 15 minutes.
- Serve warm with additional dressing, if desired.

Russian Dressing

Makes ½ cup

It only takes four ingredients to make this creamy and tangy dressing for our Reuben Swirls.

½ cup mayonnaise
3 tablespoons chili sauce*
2 tablespoons sweet pickle relish
¼ teaspoon ground black pepper

- In a small bowl, stir together mayonnaise, chili sauce, pickle relish, and pepper. Cover, and refrigerate until needed.

We used Heinz Chili Sauce.

Butternut Squash Tartlets

Makes 8

Bring the bounty of autumn's harvest to your tea table with these delectable tartlets laden with butternut squash, ground sage, and finely crumbled bacon.

1 tablespoon salted butter
½ cup sliced leeks (white part only)
1 (14.1-ounce) package refrigerated piecrust dough (2 sheets)
4 cups diced peeled butternut squash
1 tablespoon olive oil
¼ teaspoon fine sea salt
⅛ teaspoon ground black pepper
3 tablespoons salted butter, melted
1 tablespoon light brown sugar
½ teaspoon ground sage
2 tablespoons finely crumbled cooked bacon
Garnish: fresh sage leaves

- In a small sauté pan, melt 1 tablespoon butter over medium-high heat. Add leeks, and reduce heat to low. Cook, stirring frequently, until leeks are caramelized and lightly golden at edges, approximately 15 minutes. Let cool before finely chopping.
- Preheat oven to 450°.
- On a lightly floured surface, unroll piecrust dough. Using a 4½x2½-inch tartlet pan as a guide, cut 8 rectangles from pie dough. Press into bottom and up sides of 8 (4½x2½-inch) tartlet pans. Place pans on a rimmed baking sheet, and refrigerate for 30 minutes.
- Prick bottoms of tartlet shells with a fork to prevent puffing during baking.
- Bake until tartlet shells are very lightly browned, approximately 7 minutes. Let cool completely on wire racks. Carefully remove shells from tartlet pans, store in an airtight container, and use the same day.
- Reduce oven temperature to 400°. Line a rimmed baking sheet with foil.
- In a medium bowl, toss squash with olive oil, salt, and pepper to coat. Place in an even layer on prepared baking sheet.
- Bake until squash is tender, approximately 20 minutes, stirring halfway through.
- Meanwhile, in a medium bowl, stir together 3 tablespoons melted butter, brown sugar, and ground sage. Add squash, tossing gently to coat with butter mixture. Stir in caramelized leeks and bacon. Divide mixture among cooled tartlet shells.
- Garnish each tartlet with a fresh sage leaf, if desired.

MAKE-AHEAD TIP: Squash mixture can be made a day in advance, covered, and refrigerated. Gently rewarm before using, adding more butter, if needed.

MAKE-AHEAD TIP: *Bruschetta mixture can be prepared a couple of hours before serving. (Add salt just before serving, as salt can cause mixture to become watery.) Store in a covered container in the refrigerator. Fill phyllo cups just before serving.*

Assam-Vegetable Tartlets
Makes 6 (4-inch)

Goat cheese custard enrobes layers of fresh basil and a mixture of vegetables, such as shiitake mushrooms, sweet potato, and zucchini, among others, in these marvelous savory tartlets.

1 cup loosely packed chopped fresh basil, divided
Assam Tartlet Shells (recipe follows)
½ tablespoon unsalted butter
½ tablespoon olive oil
¼ cup chopped red onion
1 clove garlic, minced
¼ cup sliced shiitake mushrooms
¼ cup diced peeled sweet potato
¼ cup diced peeled carrot
¼ cup diced zucchini
¼ teaspoon fine sea salt
¼ teaspoon ground black pepper
¼ cup crumbled goat cheese
¼ cup milk
2 tablespoons heavy whipping cream
1 large egg

• Preheat oven to 375°.
• Place 2 teaspoons chopped basil in each prepared Assam Tartlet Shell.
• In a large skillet, heat butter and oil over medium heat. Stir in onion and garlic; cook until onion softens, approximately 5 minutes. Add mushrooms, sweet potato, carrot, and zucchini; cook until sweet potato is only somewhat firm, 2 to 3 minutes. Stir in salt and pepper. Remove vegetable mixture from heat. Add remaining ¾ cup basil, stirring well. Divide vegetable mixture among prepared tartlet shells.
• Sprinkle each tartlet evenly with goat cheese.
• In a small bowl, whisk together milk, cream, and egg. Divide evenly among tartlet shells.
• Bake until tartlet shells are golden and custards are set, 15 to 20 minutes. Let cool for 10 minutes before serving. Serve warm or at room temperature.

Tomato-Artichoke Bruschetta Phyllo Cups
Makes 30

Perfect for a summertime fête, these petite cups are filled with a delectable mixture of tomatoes, artichokes, and fresh oregano.

1 cup finely chopped Campari tomatoes
⅓ cup finely chopped canned artichokes
2 tablespoons red wine vinegar
1 tablespoon finely chopped fresh parsley
1 tablespoon extra-virgin olive oil
½ teaspoon finely chopped fresh oregano
⅛ teaspoon finely minced fresh garlic
¼ teaspoon ground black pepper
¼ teaspoon fine sea salt
2 (1.9-ounce) packages frozen mini phyllo cups*, thawed
Garnish: fresh oregano sprigs

• In a small bowl, stir together tomatoes, artichokes, vinegar, parsley, olive oil, oregano, garlic, pepper, and salt. Fill phyllo cups evenly with mixture.
• Garnish each cup with an oregano sprig, if desired. Serve immediately.

*We used Athen Phyllo Shells. If a crispy texture is desired, bake phyllo cups according to package directions, and let cool completely before using.

Assam Tartlet Shells
Makes 6

These sophisticated tartlet shells are imbued with Assam tea leaves and create a phenomenal vessel for a vegetable filling.

1½ cups all-purpose flour
1½ teaspoons Assam CTC black tea leaves*
½ teaspoon fine sea salt
¼ cup plus 2 tablespoons cold unsalted butter, cubed
¼ cup ice-cold water
1 large egg
1 tablespoon room temperature water

- In a large bowl, whisk together flour, tea leaves, and salt. Using a pastry blender or 2 forks, cut in cold butter until it resembles coarse crumbs. Gradually add ¼ cup ice-cold water, stirring with a fork until dry ingredients are moistened and a dough forms.
- Turn out dough onto a lightly floured surface, and shape into a disk. Wrap in plastic wrap, and refrigerate for at least 1 hour.
- Preheat oven to 375°. Spray 6 (4-inch) fluted tartlet pans with cooking spray.
- Divide dough into 6 equal pieces. On a lightly floured surface, using a rolling pin, roll out dough portions to a ⅛-inch thickness. Transfer dough to prepared tartlet pans, pressing into bottom and up sides. Using large end of a chopstick, press dough into indentations in sides of tartlet pans. Using a fork, prick bottom of dough. Place tartlet pans on a rimmed baking sheet. Top each with a piece of parchment paper, letting ends extend over edges of pans. Add pie weights or dried beans.
- Bake tartlet shells for 7 minutes. Carefully remove weights and parchment paper. Bake until crusts look dry, 4 to 5 minutes more.
- In a small bowl, whisk together egg and 1 tablespoon room temperature water to create an egg wash. Brush tartlet shells with egg wash.
- Bake for 2 minutes more. Let tartlet shells cool on a wire rack for at least 10 minutes before using.

*CTC means crush, tear, curl. Tea manufactured in this method resembles small granules similar in appearance to coffee grounds.

Shrimp Salsa Cups
Makes 12

Crispy wonton cups are the perfect vessels for a tangy salsa that features shrimp, pineapple, and two types of peppers. So the cups don't get soggy, be sure to drain the salsa well before using it and to serve immediately.

12 (3-inch-square) wonton wrappers
3 tablespoons olive oil, divided
1 tablespoon plus ½ teaspoon fine sea salt, divided
1 teaspoon fresh lime zest
2 tablespoons fresh lime juice
1 tablespoon finely diced shallot
½ pound medium fresh or thawed frozen shrimp, peeled and deveined
½ cup finely chopped red bell pepper
¼ cup finely chopped fresh pineapple
¼ cup seeded and finely chopped jalapeño pepper

• Preheat oven to 350°. Generously spray 12 alternating wells of a 24-well miniature muffin pan with cooking spray.
• Using a sharp knife, make a 1-inch slit into each edge of a wonton wrapper. Carefully press center of wonton wrapper into a prepared well. Working clockwise, fold each slit of wrapper over the next. Gently press down corners of wrapper to adhere to top of muffin tin. Repeat with remaining wonton wrappers. Brush wrappers with 2 tablespoons oil, and sprinkle with 1 tablespoon salt.
• Bake until golden brown, 5 to 8 minutes. Carefully remove wonton cups from pan and let cool completely on a wire rack.
• Heat a medium sauté pan over medium heat. In a large bowl, stir together remaining 1 tablespoon oil, remaining ½ teaspoon salt, lime zest, lime juice, and shallot. Add shrimp and stir until completely coated. Add shrimp mixture to sauté pan; cook, turning shrimp once, until pink and firm, 2 to 3 minutes. Reserving liquid from pan, remove shrimp with a slotted spoon to a cutting surface and blot shrimp dry on paper towels. Using a sharp knife, coarsely chop shrimp.
• In a medium bowl, stir together bell pepper, pineapple, and jalapeño pepper. Add chopped shrimp and enough reserved cooking liquid to slightly moisten mixture, stirring to combine. Use immediately, or cover tightly and refrigerate for a few hours until needed.
• Just before serving, drain excess liquid from shrimp salsa. Using a slotted spoon, divide shrimp salsa evenly among prepared wonton cups. Serve immediately.

Jambalaya Tartlets
Makes 12

Delicious jambalaya is creatively turned into a showstopping tartlet by filling a piecrust base with the iconic Creole chicken-and-rice mixture and topping it with shrimp and fresh parsley.

1½ (14.1-ounce) packages refrigerated piecrust dough (3 sheets)
2 tablespoons olive oil
¼ cup chopped sweet onion
¼ cup chopped green bell pepper
¼ cup chopped celery
½ cup chopped chicken thigh meat
½ cup chopped Andouille sausage
2 cups low-sodium chicken broth
1 cup long-grain rice
½ cup chopped seeded tomato
1 bay leaf
1 teaspoon chopped garlic
1 teaspoon Creole seasoning*
1 teaspoon Worcestershire sauce
½ teaspoon hot pepper sauce
½ teaspoon fine sea salt
¼ teaspoon ground black pepper
2 dozen medium shrimp, peeled and deveined, with tails on
Garnish: minced fresh parsley and 12 fresh parsley leaves

• Preheat oven to 450°.
• On a lightly floured surface, unroll piecrust dough sheets. Using a 4½x2¼-inch tartlet pan as a guide, cut 12 shapes from dough. Lightly spray 12 (4½x2¼-inch) fluted tartlet pans with cooking spray. Press dough shapes into prepared tartlet pans, trimming excess dough as necessary. Using the large end of a chopstick, press dough into indentations in sides of tartlet pans. Place tartlet pans on a rimmed baking sheet. Refrigerate for 30 minutes.
• Prick tartlet dough with a fork to prevent puffing during baking.
• Bake until tartlet shells are golden brown, approximately 7 minutes. Let cool completely on wire racks. Carefully remove shells from tartlet pans, store in an airtight container, and use the same day.
• In a large nonstick sauté pan, heat olive oil over medium-high heat. Add onion, bell pepper, celery, chicken, and sausage. Reduce heat to medium-low, and cook until vegetables are tender, stirring often. Stir in chicken broth, rice, tomato, bay leaf, garlic, Creole seasoning, Worcestershire sauce, hot pepper sauce, salt, and black pepper. Increase heat, and bring mixture to a boil. Reduce heat to a simmer, cover pan, and cook until rice is done, 15 to 20 minutes. Add shrimp to pan during the last 5 minutes of cooking time. (Shrimp are done when pink and opaque.) Spoon warm rice mixture into tartlet shells, arranging shrimp decoratively on top.
• Garnish each tartlet with minced parsley and a parsley leaf, if desired. Serve immediately.

*We used Tony Chachere's Original Creole Seasoning.

MAKE-AHEAD TIP: *Jambalaya can be made a day in advance, placed in a covered container, and refrigerated. Warm gently before filling tartlet shells.*

Muffaletta Palmiers
Makes 13

Muffaletta—a New Orleans classic sandwich made with Italian meats, cheese, and an olive salad—is transformed into a sumptuous pastry in these mouthwatering bites.

½ (17.3-ounce) package frozen puff pastry (1 sheet), slightly thawed
⅓ cup muffaletta salad*, well drained
¼ cup shredded mozzarella cheese
¼ cup shredded provolone cheese
3 tablespoons chopped genoa salami
3 tablespoons chopped capicola ham
1 large egg
1 tablespoon water

• Preheat oven to 400°. Line a rimmed baking sheet with parchment paper.
• Place puff pastry sheet on a lightly floured surface. Using a rolling pin, roll out pastry sheet slightly to flatten and make pliable.
• Blot muffaletta salad on paper towels to remove excess oil. Spread salad evenly over puff pastry, leaving a 1-inch border on each short side. Scatter cheeses over salad, and scatter meats over cheese layer. Firmly roll up both short sides of puff pastry, meeting in the center.

- Using a long, serrated knife in a gentle sawing motion, cut into ½-inch slices. Place slices 2 inches apart on prepared baking sheet.
- In a small bowl, whisk together egg and 1 tablespoon water to create an egg wash. Using a pastry brush, brush slices with egg wash.
- Bake until palmiers are golden brown, approximately 15 minutes. Serve immediately.

*Look for jars of this Italian-style olive salad on the pickle aisle of most grocery stores. We used Alpino Authentic New Orleans Style Muffaletta.

QUICHES & PASTRIES | *Teatime Savories* 57

ROAST BEEF,
TOMATO & CHEESE
TEA SANDWICHES
page 70

PRAWN SALAD
TEA SANDWICHES
page 70

CUCUMBER & MINT
CREAM CHEESE PINWHEELS
page 70

TASTY
Tea Sandwiches

WHETHER IT'S A TRADITIONAL RECIPE OR A UNIQUE SPIN ON A CLASSIC, THESE TEATIME STAPLES ARE CROWD-PLEASERS.

Duck Salad Brioche Sandwiches
Makes 16

Boneless duck breasts replace the usual chicken in the salad filling of these marvelous tea sandwiches that are studded with toasted pecans, celery, and dried cherries and are pictured with Cucumber-Tarragon Fleur-de-Lis Canapés (page 104).

1½ teaspoons olive oil
2 (7.5-ounce) boneless duck breasts
¼ cup mayonnaise
2 tablespoons chopped toasted pecans
1 tablespoon finely chopped celery
1 tablespoon chopped dried cherries
1 tablespoon coarse-grain Dijon mustard
⅛ teaspoon fine sea salt
1/16 teaspoon ground black pepper
8 slices brioche sandwich bread

- Preheat oven to 400°. Line a rimmed baking sheet with foil.
- Brush a medium sauté pan with olive oil. Heat pan over medium heat for 3 minutes.
- Using a sharp knife, score duck skin in ¼-inch intervals, being careful not to cut into duck meat. Rotate breast and score again, making a crisscross pattern.
- Place duck breasts skin side down in heated pan, cover, and cook for 10 minutes. Turn breasts over and cook for 2 minutes. Transfer duck to prepared rimmed baking sheet, skin side up.
- Bake duck for 13 minutes. Let cool for 30 minutes.
- Remove and discard skin. Using a sharp knife, coarsely chop duck. Place chopped duck in the work bowl of a food processor. Pulse until finely chopped.
- In a medium bowl, stir together duck, mayonnaise, pecans, celery, cherries, mustard, salt, and pepper until thoroughly combined.
- Spread a thick, even layer of duck salad onto 4 brioche slices. Top each with a remaining brioche slice to make 4 whole sandwiches.
- Using a serrated bread knife in a gentle sawing motion, trim and discard crusts from sandwiches, creating perfect 3¼-inch squares. Cut each sandwich diagonally into 4 equal triangles. Serve immediately, or cover with damp paper towels, place in a covered container, refrigerate, and serve within 2 hours.

MAKE-AHEAD TIP: Duck salad can be made a day in advance, stored in a covered container, and refrigerated.

Earl Grey Chicken Salad Tea Sandwiches
Makes 36

Globally the most popular flavored black tea, Earl Grey is used here in two different ways—steeped in heavy cream that is used as the filling's binder and added as loose tea to the filling itself—to elevate traditional chicken salad. Be sure to use a brand of tea that offers a double-bergamot version so the iconic taste will be noticeable on the first bite.

1⅓ cups heavy whipping cream
6 double-bergamot Earl Grey tea bags*, divided
1 teaspoon granulated sugar
½ teaspoon fine sea salt
¼ teaspoon ground black pepper
3 cups coarsely chopped roasted chicken**
⅓ cup chopped green grapes
2 tablespoons finely chopped celery
2 tablespoons chopped toasted unblanched almonds
1 tablespoon finely chopped fresh tarragon
⅓ cup mayonnaise
18 slices potato bread

- In a small saucepan, heat cream over medium-high heat until very hot, steaming, and bubbles form around edge of pan. Remove pan from heat. Add 5 tea bags, and cover pan. Let steep for 5 minutes. Remove tea bags from cream, and place in a fine-mesh sieve over saucepan. Press tea bags over steeped cream to extract any remaining cream. Stir in sugar, salt, and pepper until combined. Let cool completely.
- Place chopped chicken in the work bowl of a food processor. Pulse a few times until chicken is finely chopped, being very careful not to over-process chicken.
- In a large bowl, stir together finely chopped chicken, grapes, celery, almonds, tarragon, and steeped cream. Stir in 1 teaspoon loose tea from remaining tea bag. Stir mixture together thoroughly until combined. Cover and refrigerate until flavors meld, at least 4 hours and up to a day.
- Spread a thin layer of mayonnaise onto bread slices. Spread chicken salad in a thick, even layer onto 9 bread slices. Top each with a remaining bread slice, mayonnaise side down, to make 9 whole sandwiches.
- Using a serrated bread knife in a gentle sawing motion, trim and discard crusts from sandwiches. Cut each sandwich into 4 equal rectangles, creating 36 tea sandwiches. Serve immediately, or cover with damp paper towels, place in a covered container, refrigerate, and serve within 4 hours.

*We used Stash Double Bergamot Earl Grey Black Tea.
**For best flavor, we used white and dark meat from an unseasoned rotisserie chicken.

- Using a 3-tablespoon levered scoop, portion ham mixture onto 5 bread slices. Spread ham mixture in a thick, even layer. Top ham layer with a layer of lettuce. Top each with a remaining bread slice to make 5 whole sandwiches.
- Using a serrated bread knife in a gentle sawing motion, trim and discard crusts from sandwiches, creating even squares. Cut each sandwich diagonally into 4 equal triangles. Serve immediately, or cover with damp paper towels, place in a covered container, refrigerate, and serve within 2 hours.

Cucumber–Herbed Cheese Tea Sandwiches
Makes 12

Shallot-and-chive–flavored Gournay cheese imparts creamy and herbaceous flavor to refreshing cucumbers in this simple, yet marvelous, light bite.

6 slices very thin white sandwich bread, frozen
1 (5.2-ounce) package shallot-and-chive–flavored Gournay cheese*, room temperature
1 (6-inch) section English cucumber with peel, finely chopped

- Using a 2⅛-inch flower-shaped cutter, cut 24 shapes from frozen bread slices, discarding scraps. Using a ¾-inch round cutter, cut centers from 12 flower shapes, discarding scraps.
- Place cheese in a piping bag fitted with a medium round tip (Wilton #12), and pipe cheese around edges of 12 solid bread flowers, filling centers. Top each with a bread flower with a center cutout to make 12 sandwiches. Place sandwiches in a resealable plastic bag, or cover with damp paper towels while bread defrosts to prevent sandwiches from drying out.
- Just before serving, fill centers of tea sandwiches with chopped cucumber.

*We used Boursin Shallot & Chive spreadable cheese.

MAKE-AHEAD TIP: Flower shapes can be cut from bread a day in advance and stored in a resealable plastic bag to retain freshness. Sandwiches can be assembled a few hours in advance, covered with damp paper towels, and stored in an airtight container in the refrigerator until serving time.

Ham-and-Egg Salad Tea Sandwiches
Makes 20

The addition of chopped ham not only makes traditional egg salad tastier but also a bit heartier for the savories course of afternoon tea.

4 cups chopped cooked ham
1 cup mayonnaise
2 large hard-cooked eggs, finely chopped
⅓ cup finely chopped celery
¼ cup spicy brown mustard
3 tablespoons dill pickle relish
¼ teaspoon ground black pepper
10 slices firm white sandwich bread, frozen
2 cups chopped butter lettuce

- In the work bowl of a food processor, pulse ham until finely ground.
- In a large bowl, stir together ham, mayonnaise, eggs, celery, mustard, pickle relish, and pepper.

Prosciutto, Pesto & Black-Eyed Pea Hummus Tea Sandwiches

Makes 9

Since many people will dutifully eat black-eyed peas, greens, and ham on New Year's Day in hopes that the combination will bring prosperity for the year, this marvelous tea sandwich presents the traditional food trio in afternoon-tea–friendly fashion and is pictured with Roast Beef Croissants (opposite page) and Herbed Deviled Eggs (page 119).

1 (15.8-ounce) can black-eyed peas, rinsed and drained
1 tablespoon fresh lemon juice
1 tablespoon extra-virgin olive oil
1 clove garlic, chopped
¼ teaspoon fine sea salt
¼ teaspoon ground cumin
2 tablespoons tahini
1 tablespoon water
6 slices white bread, frozen
3 tablespoons prepared refrigerated pesto
9 thin slices prosciutto

- In the work bowl of a food processor, pulse together black-eyed peas, lemon juice, olive oil, garlic, salt, and cumin until smooth. With processor running, add tahini and 1 tablespoon water, processing until smooth. Transfer hummus to a covered container and refrigerate for at least 1 hour.
- Using a serrated bread knife in a gentle sawing motion, trim and discard crusts from frozen bread slices to create 3-inch squares. Cut each bread square into 3 (3x1-inch) rectangles.
- Spread a thin layer of pesto onto bread rectangles.
- Transfer chilled hummus to a piping bag fitted with a small French star tip (Ateco #866). Pipe hummus onto pesto side of 9 bread rectangles.
- Using a sharp knife, cut 18 (3x1-inch) strips from prosciutto. Place 2 prosciutto strips over each hummus layer. Top with remaining bread rectangles, pesto side down, to make 9 tea sandwiches. Cover with damp paper towels, and let bread thaw before serving; or cover with damp paper towels, place in a covered container, refrigerate, and serve within an hour.

KITCHEN TIP: To make sure cuts are straight, place bread slices on a gridded cutting surface or on a gridded cooling rack.

Roast Beef Croissants
Makes 12

The woodsy and aromatic notes of a homemade rosemary butter impart tremendous flavor to this hearty roast beef sandwich that just might become your new go-to for teatime—and maybe for lunch as well. It is pictured, opposite page, with Prosciutto, Pesto & Black-Eyed Pea Hummus Tea Sandwiches and Herbed Deviled Eggs (page 119).

¼ cup unsalted butter, room temperature
1 teaspoon finely chopped fresh rosemary
1 cup baby arugula, stemmed
2 teaspoons olive oil
⅛ teaspoon fine sea salt
12 mini croissants*
6 thin slices deli roast beef, halved lengthwise

- In a small bowl, stir together butter and rosemary.
- In a medium bowl, toss together arugula, olive oil, and salt.
- Using a serrated bread knife in a gentle sawing motion, cut croissants almost in half horizontally.
- Spread butter mixture onto cut surfaces of croissants. Fill each croissant with a few sprigs of arugula and a roast beef piece. Serve immediately, or cover with damp paper towels, place in a covered container, refrigerate, and serve within 2 hours.

*If baked mini croissants are not available in your grocery store, ask the bakery department manager if you can purchase unbaked mini croissants to bake at home.

Turkey-Swiss Roulades
Makes 24 to 28 slices

A simple teatime sandwich of swirled meat and cheese is thoughtfully crafted to resemble a saucer hat with the help of an arugula-garnish plume and is pictured here with Beanie Flatbread Hummus Bites (page 110).

4 ounces cream cheese, softened
½ tablespoon dry ranch dip mix
2 (9-inch) whole-wheat flour tortillas
½ cup shredded Swiss cheese
4 slices deli-style roast turkey
Garnish: arugula

- In a small bowl, beat together cream cheese and dip mix with a mixer at medium speed until smooth.
- Using a small offset spatula, spread half of cream cheese mixture in an even layer onto each tortilla. Sprinkle each tortilla with ¼ cup Swiss cheese, and arrange turkey on top of cheese.
- Starting at one end, roll up each tortilla, jelly roll style, encasing ingredients and ending with seam side down. Wrap tightly in plastic wrap, and refrigerate for at least 30 minutes and up to 2 days.
- When ready to serve, unwrap roulades. Using a serrated knife, cut ends off each roulade to neaten. Cut roulades into ½-inch slices.
- Garnish each slice with arugula to resemble a plume, if desired. Serve immediately.

Date & Roasted Chicken Salad Tea Sandwiches
Makes 30

Chopped dates and toasted pecans give traditional chicken salad an unexpected upgrade in these delightful sandwiches, which are pictured with Smoked Salmon Blini (page 108) and Caramelized Leek & Pancetta Quiche (page 33).

9 tablespoons mayonnaise, divided
1 tablespoon sherry vinegar
¼ teaspoon fine sea salt
⅛ teaspoon ground black pepper
2 cups finely chopped roast chicken (white and dark meat)
¼ cup chopped pitted dates
¼ cup coarsely chopped toasted pecans
2½ tablespoons finely chopped celery
20 slices firm honey wheat bread, frozen
¾ cup loosely packed, chopped baby arugula

- In a large bowl, whisk together 6 tablespoons mayonnaise, vinegar, salt, and pepper until combined. Stir in chicken, dates, pecans, and celery, stirring until well combined.
- Using a 2-inch triangular cutter, cut 3 triangles from each frozen bread slice, discarding scraps. To prevent bread from drying out during assembly, cover with damp paper towels, or store in a resealable plastic bag.
- Spread a thin layer of remaining 3 tablespoons mayonnaise onto bread triangles. Hold the slightly damp same cutter over 1 bread triangle, mayonnaise side up; layer 1 teaspoon arugula and 1 tablespoon chicken salad, spreading to points and pressing salad down slightly to fit shape. Remove cutter. Top with a remaining bread triangle, mayonnaise side down. Repeat with remaining ingredients to make 30 tea sandwiches. Serve immediately, or cover with damp paper towels, place in a covered container, refrigerate, and serve within 2 hours.

MAKE-AHEAD TIP: Chicken salad can be made a day in advance, stored in a covered container, and refrigerated until needed.

Curried Shrimp & Mango Salad Tea Sandwiches
Makes 12

Warm spice from curry powder mingles effortlessly with shrimp, cilantro, lime juice, and fresh mango in this golden-hued salad that fills these fantastic tea sandwiches. If you enjoy curried chicken salad, then you will appreciate this inventive take on the classic, with seafood and fruit adding marvelous flavor. These sandwiches are pictured with Ham & Pineapple Pinwheels (below right) and Strawberry & Goat Cheese Crostini (page 92).

1 pound medium shrimp, peeled and deveined
2 teaspoons olive oil
1 teaspoon curry powder
½ cup finely chopped fresh ripe mango, blotted dry on paper towels
5 tablespoons mayonnaise
2 tablespoons finely chopped red bell pepper
2 tablespoons finely chopped fresh cilantro
1 teaspoon fresh lime zest
2 teaspoons fresh lime juice
½ teaspoon fine sea salt
¼ teaspoon ground black pepper
12 large slices hearty white sandwich bread, frozen

• Preheat oven to 350°. Line a rimmed baking sheet with parchment paper.
• In a medium bowl, toss shrimp with olive oil and curry powder. Arrange in a single layer on prepared baking sheet.
• Bake until shrimp are pink and firm, 8 to 10 minutes. When shrimp are cool enough to handle, chop finely.
• In a medium bowl, stir together chopped shrimp, mango, mayonnaise, bell pepper, cilantro, lime zest, lime juice, salt, and black pepper. Transfer salad to a covered container, and refrigerate until cold, approximately 4 hours.
• Using a 2-inch square cutter, cut 24 squares from frozen bread slices, discarding scraps. To prevent bread from drying out during assembly, cover with damp paper towels, or store in a resealable plastic bag.
• Spread 2 tablespoons shrimp salad onto 12 bread squares. Top each with a remaining bread square to make 12 tea sandwiches. Serve immediately, or cover with damp paper towels, place in a covered container, refrigerate, and serve within 2 hours.

Ham & Pineapple Pinwheels
Makes 24

This crowd-pleasing, delicious recipe boasts pineapple in two different forms. The tropical ingredient melds beautifully with ham, arugula, and Dijon mustard in this modest savory, which is pictured with Curried Shrimp & Mango Salad Tea Sandwiches (left) and Strawberry & Goat Cheese Crostini (page 92).

4 ounces cream cheese, softened
2 tablespoons finely chopped dried pineapple
1 tablespoon pineapple preserves
1 tablespoon Dijon mustard
3 large flour tortillas
9 thin slices deli ham
1½ ounces arugula or spinach
Garnish: additional pineapple preserves

• In a small bowl, stir together cream cheese, dried pineapple, pineapple preserves, and mustard.
• Spread 3 tablespoons cream cheese mixture onto each tortilla. Place 3 ham slices over cream cheese layer on each tortilla. Top ham layer with an even layer of arugula or spinach.
• Roll up tortillas tightly. Wrap each tortilla in plastic wrap, and refrigerate for at least an hour and up to a day.
• Just before serving, unwrap tortillas and place on a cutting surface. Using a serrated knife in a gentle sawing motion, trim and discard ends from each tortilla. Cut each tortilla into 8 slices.
• Garnish slices with a dollop of pineapple preserves, if desired. Serve immediately.

Roast Lamb Salad Tea Sandwiches with Pistachio-Mint Pesto

Makes 9

Grass-fed lamb, perfectly seasoned with an array of herbs and spices, is the key to these tasty tea sandwiches, which are pictured with Cucumber-Watercress Canapés (page 113).

1 (1.21-pound) Frenched rack of grass-fed lamb
¼ teaspoon garlic salt
⅜ teaspoon ground black pepper, divided
¼ teaspoon minced fresh rosemary
¼ teaspoon crushed dried oregano
2 teaspoons extra-virgin olive oil
4 tablespoons mayonnaise, divided
1 teaspoon yellow mustard
⅛ teaspoon fine sea salt
2 tablespoons unsalted butter, softened
6 slices brioche sandwich bread
Pistachio-Mint Pesto (recipe follows)
1 cup chopped butter lettuce

- Using a sharp knife, cut away silver skin from lamb, if necessary. Season all sides of lamb with garlic salt, ¼ teaspoon pepper, rosemary, and oregano. Wrap seasoned lamb well in foil and refrigerate overnight.
- Preheat oven to 450°.
- Unwrap lamb and place on a rimmed baking sheet, ribs curving down, meat side up.
- Roast lamb in the oven until an instant-read meat thermometer registers 145°, approximately 30 minutes. Let meat cool for 30 minutes.
- Using a sharp knife, cut lamb rack between rib bones into chops. (If meat is too pink, brush a sauté pan with olive oil, heat pan, and sear lamb chops just until pink is gone and meat is lightly browned, being careful not to overcook lamb.) Cut meat away from bones into lamb medallions. Coarsely chop meat. (This should yield approximately 1⅓ cups chopped meat.)
- Place chopped meat in the work bowl of a food processor. Pulse a few times until meat is finely chopped, being very careful not to overprocess meat.
- In a medium bowl, stir together finely chopped meat, 3 tablespoons mayonnaise, mustard, salt, and remaining ⅛ teaspoon ground pepper until combined. Stir in remaining 1 tablespoon mayonnaise, if needed, to achieve a spreadable consistency.
- Spread a thin layer of butter onto 6 brioche slices. Spread an even layer of Pistachio-Mint Pesto over butter. Spread a thick even layer of lamb salad over pesto on 3 brioche slices. Cover lamb with an even layer of lettuce. Top each lettuce layer with remaining 3 brioche slices, pesto side down, to make 3 whole sandwiches.
- Using a serrated bread knife in a gentle sawing motion, trim and discard crusts from sandwiches. Cut each sandwich into 3 rectangles to yield a total of 9 finger sandwiches. Serve immediately, or cover with damp paper towels, place in a covered container, and refrigerate for a few hours until serving time.

Pistachio-Mint Pesto

Makes ½ cup

For a perfect complement to the lamb in our Roast Lamb Salad Tea Sandwiches, fresh mint and parsley replace the usual basil in this pesto, which uses pistachios instead of the traditional pine nuts.

2 (.5-ounce) packages fresh mint leaves (1 cup loosely packed)
⅓ cup loosely packed flat-leaf parsley leaves
⅓ cup roasted unsalted pistachios
1 tablespoon fresh lemon juice
¼ cup finely grated Parmesan cheese*
¼ cup plus ½ teaspoon extra-virgin olive oil, divided
⅛ teaspoon fine sea salt
1 pinch ground black pepper

- Remove and discard stems from mint and parsley.
- In the work bowl of a food processor, pulse together mint, parsley, pistachios, lemon juice, cheese, ¼ cup olive oil, salt, and pepper until somewhat smooth.
- Transfer pesto to a small glass container. Drizzle remaining ½ teaspoon oil on surface of pesto. Place a piece of plastic wrap directly onto pesto. Refrigerate until needed. Stir pesto before using.

*We used a Microplane zester to achieve a light, wispy texture.

MAKE-AHEAD TIP: Pistachio-Mint Pesto can be made up to a day in advance. Stir pesto before using.

Prawn Salad Tea Sandwiches
Makes 12

"Prawn" is a term the British use to refer to all shrimp as well as to true prawns. Either of these crustaceans will work equally well in these lovely tea sandwiches.

1 pound peeled, deveined, and cooked prawns or shrimp
⅓ cup mayonnaise
1 teaspoon fresh lemon juice
½ teaspoon fine sea salt
⅛ teaspoon ground black pepper
½ cup coarsely chopped watercress
6 large slices honey wheat bread

- In the work bowl of a food processor, pulse prawns until finely chopped.
- In a medium bowl, stir together mayonnaise, lemon juice, salt, and pepper until combined. Stir in watercress and prawns. Transfer prawn salad to a covered container and refrigerate until cold, several hours and up to a day.
- Spread prawn salad in a thick, even layer onto 3 bread slices. Top each with a remaining bread slice to make 3 whole sandwiches.
- Using a serrated bread knife in a gentle sawing motion, trim and discard crusts from sandwiches to make even squares. Cut each sandwich diagonally into 4 equal triangles. Serve immediately, or cover with damp paper towels, place in a covered container, and refrigerate for up to 2 hours until serving time.

Roast Beef, Tomato & Cheese Tea Sandwiches
Makes 12

A truly English flavor combination, roast beef with tomato and Cheddar cheese is sure to please, especially in dainty sandwiches for teatime.

¼ cup unsalted butter, softened
8 slices white sandwich bread
2 medium beefsteak tomatoes, peeled*
1 cup finely shredded white Cheddar cheese
16 thin slices deli-style roast beef

- Spread a thin layer of butter onto each bread slice.
- Using a sharp knife, cut each tomato into quarters. Carefully remove seeds and membrane inside each piece. Cut each quarter into 4 (¾-inch-wide) strips.
- Arrange ¼ cup cheese, 8 tomato strips, and 4 roast beef slices onto butter side of each of 4 bread slices. Top each with a remaining bread slice, butter side down, to make 4 whole sandwiches.
- Using a serrated bread knife in a gentle sawing motion, trim and discard crusts from sandwiches to create 4½x3-inch rectangles. Cut each sandwich into 3 (3x1½-inch) rectangles. Serve immediately, or cover with damp paper towels, place in a covered container, and refrigerate for a few hours until serving time.

*Although there are many ways to peel a tomato, one of the easiest is to slightly pierce its skin and then to submerge the tomato in boiling water just long enough for the skin to burst. Quickly plunge the tomato in iced water to stop the cooking process. Remove and discard skin.

Cucumber & Mint Cream Cheese Pinwheels
Makes 15

Slices of fresh cucumber and a spread of mint-laced cream cheese are the fillings for these petite sandwich-bread pinwheels. They are so good and refreshing that guests might have a difficult time limiting themselves to just one.

3 slices firm white sandwich bread
2 ounces (¼ cup) cream cheese, softened
1 teaspoon minced fresh mint
½ teaspoon fresh lemon zest
½ teaspoon fresh lemon juice
1 dash fine sea salt
1 English cucumber

- Trim crusts from long edges of bread slices.
- In a small bowl, stir together cream cheese, mint, lemon zest, lemon juice, and salt.
- Using a vegetable peeler, shave 15 (5x1¼-inch) lengthwise strips from cucumber.
- Using a rolling pin, roll white bread slices to a ¼-inch thickness. Divide cream cheese mixture among bread slices. Spread cream cheese into a thin, even layer over bread slices. Starting on one long side, shingle 5 cucumber slices on top of cream cheese, trimming as necessary.

Starting on a long end, roll up bread jelly roll style to encase cucumber and cream cheese. Wrap each log tightly in plastic wrap and refrigerate for at least an hour.
• Just before serving, unwrap logs and place on a cutting surface. Using a thin, serrated bread knife in a gentle sawing motion, trim and discard ends to make 5-inch-long logs. Cut each log into 5 (1-inch) slices. Serve immediately.

TEA SANDWICHES | *Teatime Savories*

frozen bread slices, discarding scraps. To prevent bread from drying out during assembly, cover with damp paper towels, or store in a resealable plastic bag.
• Spread a thin layer of pesto onto each bread round. Pipe cheese mixture onto pesto side of 12 bread rounds, and sprinkle with remaining ¼ cup pecans. Top each with a remaining bread round, pesto side down. Serve immediately, or cover with damp paper towels, place in a covered container, refrigerate, and serve within an hour. For best flavor, let come to room temperature before serving.

MAKE-AHEAD TIP: *Pesto can be made a day in advance. Place pesto in a covered container, coat top of pesto with a thin layer of olive oil, and refrigerate. When ready to use, stir olive oil into pesto. Bread rounds can be cut a day in advance and stored in a resealable plastic bag to prevent drying out.*

Arugula-Pecan Pesto & Goat Cheese Tea Sandwiches
Makes 12

A homemade pesto of fresh arugula, Parmesan cheese, and toasted pecans combines with two other types of cheese to fill these tasty tea sandwiches.

½ (4-ounce) package fresh baby arugula
½ cup chopped toasted pecans, divided
¼ cup finely grated Parmesan cheese
1 tablespoon extra-virgin olive oil
1 teaspoon red wine vinegar
⅛ teaspoon fine sea salt
⅛ teaspoon ground black pepper
⅛ teaspoon garlic powder
1 (8-ounce) package goat cheese, room temperature
1 (3-ounce) package cream cheese, softened
12 slices honey wheat bread, frozen

• In the work bowl of a food processor, pulse together arugula, ¼ cup pecans, Parmesan cheese, olive oil, vinegar, salt, pepper, and garlic powder until arugula is finely chopped and ingredients are well blended.
• In a medium bowl, beat together goat cheese and cream cheese with a mixer at medium-high speed. Transfer cheese mixture to a pastry bag fitted with a large open star tip (Wilton #1M).
• Using a 1¾-inch round cutter, cut 24 rounds from

Creole Filet Tea Sandwiches
Makes 8

Slices of tender filet mignon are accompanied by baby kale and homemade Creole Mustard Butter on sourdough bread to fashion a hearty tea sandwich that is sure to please a hungry crowd. For additional color and flavor, garnish with petite slices of grape tomato. Tea sandwiches are pictured with Crab Cake Crostini (page 94).

1 (8-ounce) beef filet mignon steak
¼ teaspoon garlic salt
¼ teaspoon fresh ground black pepper
2 teaspoons extra-virgin olive oil, divided
4 slices bakery-style sourdough bread
Creole Mustard Butter (recipe follows)
½ cup baby kale
Garnish: grape tomato slices

• Season all sides of steak evenly with garlic salt and pepper. Drizzle with 1 teaspoon olive oil and rub in with fingers. Let steak sit at room temperature for 30 minutes.
• In a small sauté pan, heat remaining 1 teaspoon oil over medium-high heat. When pan and oil are hot, place steak in pan, reduce heat to medium, and cook, undisturbed, until well seared, 5 to 7 minutes. Turn steak over and cook until desired doneness is achieved, 3 to 5 minutes for rare. Wrap steak securely in foil and let rest until cool.*

- Using a serrated bread knife in a gentle sawing motion, cut 16 (2½x1-inch) rectangles from bread slices, discarding scraps. Place bread rectangles in a resealable plastic bag to prevent drying out during assembly.
- Spread an even layer of Creole Mustard Butter onto bread rectangles. On butter side of 8 bread rectangles, arrange a layer of kale. Using a sharp knife, cut 8 thin slices from steak to fit bread rectangles. Blot steak strips on paper towels to absorb juices before placing on top of kale. Cover each with a remaining bread rectangle, butter side down. Serve immediately, or cover with damp paper towels, place in a covered container, refrigerate, and serve within 2 hours.
- Just before serving, garnish with grape tomato slices, if desired.

*At this point, steak can be refrigerated. Use within 2 days.

Creole Mustard Butter
Makes approximately ¼ cup

Four ingredients make up this flavorful butter that combines Creole mustard, parsley, and thyme into one tasty and herbaceous condiment for tea sandwiches.

4 tablespoons unsalted butter, softened
2 tablespoons Creole mustard*
1 teaspoon finely chopped fresh parsley
½ teaspoon chopped fresh thyme

- In a small bowl, stir together butter, mustard, parsley, and thyme. Use immediately, or cover, refrigerate, and use within a day. Let come to room temperature before using.

*We used Zatarain's Creole Mustard.

- Using a 1½-inch fluted round cutter, cut 24 rounds from frozen bread slices, discarding scraps. To prevent bread from drying out during assembly, cover with damp paper towels, or store in a resealable plastic bag.
- Using a sharp knife, cut off and discard green tops and roots from radishes. Using a sharp knife or a mandoline, cut 24 very thin slices from radishes, discarding small end slices.
- In a small bowl, stir together butter, dill, basil, parsley, and lemon juice until combined.
- Using an offset spatula, spread an even layer of butter mixture onto 24 bread rounds. Place 2 radish slices on butter side of 12 bread rounds. Top each with a remaining bread round, butter side down. Serve immediately, or cover with damp paper towels, place in a covered container, and refrigerate for up to an hour before serving.
- Just before serving, garnish with radish microgreens, if desired.

*We used Micro Radish Mix from Gourmet Sweet Botanicals, 800-931-7530, gourmetsweetbotanicals.com.

Chilled Crab Salad Sandwiches
Makes 20

Herbaceous crab salad and fresh watercress on honey wheat bread is a delectable savory combination for afternoon tea and is pictured with Radish & Herbed Butter Sandwiches (left) and Mushroom-Leek Quiche Squares (page 32).

8 ounces lump crabmeat, picked for shell
2 cups iced water
1 tablespoon plus 1 teaspoon fresh lemon juice, divided
⅓ cup mayonnaise
2 teaspoons chopped flat-leaf parsley
2 teaspoons chopped green onion (green tops only)
1 teaspoon chopped tarragon
1 teaspoon prepared English mustard
¼ teaspoon fine sea salt
⅛ teaspoon celery seed
⅛ teaspoon ground white pepper
⅛ teaspoon ground black pepper
10 slices firm honey wheat bread
2 cups watercress

- Place crabmeat in a bowl. Cover with 2 cups iced water combined with 1 tablespoon lemon juice. Let sit for 1 minute. Using a fine-mesh sieve, drain crabmeat.

Radish & Herbed Butter Sandwiches
Makes 12

A sumptuous butter laced with dill, basil, parsley, and a hint of lemon pairs well with the bright flavor and texture of a thin layer of radishes in these tea sandwiches, shown here with Chilled Crab Tea Sandwiches (right) and Mushroom-Leek Quiche Squares (page 32).

12 slices firm white sandwich bread, frozen
1 to 2 bunches multicolor radishes with green tops
¼ cup salted butter, room temperature
1 tablespoon finely chopped fresh dill
1 teaspoon finely chopped fresh basil
½ teaspoon finely chopped flat-leaf parsley
1 teaspoon fresh lemon juice
Garnish: radish microgreens*

Remove crabmeat from sieve. Line sieve with paper towels and drain crabmeat again.
• In a medium bowl, stir together mayonnaise, parsley, green onion, tarragon, mustard, remaining 1 teaspoon lemon juice, salt, celery seed, and peppers. Using a fork, gently stir in drained crabmeat so it does not shred.
• Spread a thick, even layer of chilled crab salad onto 5 bread slices. Top evenly with watercress and with a remaining bread slice to make 5 whole sandwiches.
• Using a serrated bread knife in a gentle sawing motion, trim and discard crusts from sandwiches, creating perfect 3-inch square sandwiches. Cut each sandwich diagonally into 4 equal triangles. Serve immediately, or cover with damp paper towels, place in a covered container, and refrigerate for up to an hour before serving.

MAKE-AHEAD TIP: *Crab salad can be made up to a day in advance, stored in a covered container, and refrigerated.*

Lobster "Spring Roll" Tea Sandwiches
Makes 12

Rice-based bread, steamed lobster, shredded carrots, and fresh basil combine in this innovative and elevated take on an Asian spring roll. Shingle three slices of cocktail cucumber on top of each seaside-inspired sandwich for an attractive presentation.

¼ cup creamy peanut butter
1 tablespoon rice vinegar
1 tablespoon tamari soy sauce
1 tablespoon honey
½ teaspoon grated fresh garlic
2 tablespoons mayonnaise
1 tablespoon fresh lemon juice
1 teaspoon hot pepper sauce
½ teaspoon fine sea salt
½ pound lobster tails, cooked, shells removed, and finely chopped*
¼ cup coarsely grated carrot**
2 tablespoons finely chopped fresh basil
2 cocktail cucumbers
24 slices gluten-free rice-based bread***, frozen

• In a small bowl, whisk together peanut butter, vinegar, soy sauce, honey, and garlic until well combined.
• In a medium bowl, whisk together mayonnaise, lemon juice, hot pepper sauce, and salt. Add lobster, carrot, and basil, tossing to combine.
• Using a mandoline, slice cucumbers into 1/16-inch-thick rounds. Reserve 36 slices for garnish.
• Using a large knife, trim and discard crusts from each frozen bread slice to make 24 (2½x1¼inch) rectangles. Place bread in a resealable plastic bag to let thaw and prevent drying out during assembly.
• Spread a thin layer of peanut butter mixture onto bread rectangles. On peanut butter side of 12 bread rectangles, shingle 3 or 4 cucumber slices. Spread approximately 2 teaspoons lobster mixture each onto cucumber layer. Top with remaining 12 bread rectangles, peanut butter side down. Serve immediately, or cover with damp paper towels, place in a covered container, refrigerate, and serve within 2 hours.
• Just before serving, garnish sandwiches with 3 reserved cucumber slices each.

*Most seafood departments at grocery stores will steam the tails upon request.
**We used the large holes of box grater.
***We used Canyon Bakehouse Mountain white bread. We recommend purchasing two loaves of bread in case some slices have large holes that would make them difficult to use fully.

On mayonnaise side of 12 bread squares, spread 1 tablespoon crab mixture each, top with a small amount of watercress, and cover with remaining bread squares, mayonnaise side down, to make 12 sandwiches. Serve immediately, or cover with damp paper towels, place in a covered container, refrigerate, and serve within an hour.

Honey Ham & Dijon Tea Sandwiches
Makes 8

The peppery bite of fresh watercress is an ideal complement to the ham and other ingredients of this simple tea sandwich, which is pictured with Smoked Salmon & Caper Cream Cheese–Filled Cucumber Canapés (page 102) and Mini Zucchini Quiches (page 34).

8 slices white sandwich bread, frozen
1 tablespoon plus 1 teaspoon mayonnaise
1 tablespoon plus 1 teaspoon stone-ground Dijon mustard
3 tablespoons unsalted butter, softened
8 very thin slices honey ham*
½ cup loosely packed watercress
Garnish: watercress

• Using a 2-inch square cutter, cut 16 squares from frozen bread slices, discarding scraps. To prevent bread from drying out during assembly, cover with damp paper towels, or store in a resealable plastic bag, and let thaw at room temperature.
• In a small bowl, stir together mayonnaise and mustard. Spread a layer of mixture onto 8 bread squares. Spread a layer of butter onto remaining 8 bread squares. Fold each ham slice in half, and place on top of mayonnaise spread side of bread squares, gathering and folding ham to ruffle it and trimming ham to fit, if necessary. Top ham with watercress and cover with remaining bread squares, butter side down.
• Garnish with watercress, if desired.

*If ham has excess moisture, pat dry with paper towels.

MAKE-AHEAD TIPS: *Bread squares can be cut a day in advance and stored in a resealable plastic bag. Sandwiches can be assembled earlier in the day, covered with damp paper towels, placed in a covered container, and refrigerated. Garnish just before serving.*

Crab Tea Sandwiches
Makes 12

Inspired by the fresh seafood available along the Cornish coast of England, these crab sandwiches are laced with the bright notes of fresh lemon, parsley, and dill.

12 slices multigrain bread, frozen
1 (8-ounce) container lump crabmeat, drained and picked for shell
1 teaspoon chopped fresh parsley
1 teaspoon chopped fresh dill
1 teaspoon olive oil
¼ teaspoon fine sea salt
¼ teaspoon paprika
3 tablespoons mayonnaise
1 tablespoon Dijon mustard
¼ teaspoon lightly packed fresh lemon zest
1½ teaspoons fresh lemon juice
Watercress

• Using a 2¼-inch square cutter, cut 24 squares from frozen bread slices, discarding scraps. To prevent bread from drying out during assembly, place bread squares in a resealable plastic bag, and let thaw.
• In a small bowl, gently stir together crabmeat, parsley, dill, olive oil, salt, and paprika.
• In another small bowl, stir together mayonnaise, mustard, lemon zest, and lemon juice. Spread a layer of mayonnaise mixture onto each bread square.

76 | Teatime Savories | TEA SANDWICHES

Egg & Cress Tea Sandwiches
Makes 12

Elevate a classic egg mayonnaise (egg salad) with watercress, a quintessentially British green that can also make for charming garnish for a number of savories. Slices of soft, tender brioche bread are the perfect vessels for this sandwich filling, pictured with Garden Vegetable, Roast Beef & Cheddar Tea Sandwiches (right) and Salmon Roses on Cucumber Rounds (page 94).

6 large eggs, hard-cooked and peeled
¾ cup finely chopped watercress
½ cup mayonnaise
2 tablespoons coarse-ground Dijon mustard
1 teaspoon finely chopped fresh dill
¼ teaspoon fine sea salt
⅛ teaspoon ground white pepper
8 slices brioche sandwich bread

• In a medium bowl, using a pastry blender or 2 forks, chop eggs into small pieces. Add watercress, mayonnaise, mustard, dill, salt, and pepper, stirring to blend.
• Spread a thick layer of egg mixture onto 4 bread slices. Top each with a remaining bread slice to make 4 whole sandwiches.
• Using a serrated bread knife in a gentle sawing motion, trim and discard crusts from sandwiches. Cut sandwiches into 3 rectangles. Serve immediately, or cover with damp paper towels, place in a covered container, refrigerate, and serve within an hour.

MAKE-AHEAD TIP: Egg mayonnaise (egg salad) can be made without watercress up to a day in advance, placed in a covered container, and refrigerated. Add watercress just before using.

Garden Vegetable, Roast Beef & Cheddar Tea Sandwiches
Makes 12

Fresh vegetables pickled in a vinegar mixture are piquant additions to finger sandwiches layered with a Savoury Aïoli, spinach leaves, roast beef, and Cheddar cheese. They are pictured with Egg & Cress Tea Sandwiches (left) and Salmon Roses on Cucumber Rounds (page 94).

1 medium yellow courgette (summer squash)*
1 medium golden beetroot
2 thin slices shallot
1 cup sherry vinegar
½ teaspoon granulated sugar
Savoury Aïoli (recipe follows)
8 slices seedless rye bread
1 cup loosely packed baby spinach leaves
4 ultra-thin slices Cheddar cheese
16 thin slices deli-style roast beef

• Using a Y-shaped vegetable peeler, cut thin vertical strips from courgette, approximately 12 slices. Peel beetroot, discarding skin. Cut approximately 24 slices from beetroot. Place courgette, beetroot, and shallot slices in a bowl and cover with vinegar and sugar. Toss vegetables in vinegar mixture. Let sit at room temperature until softened, 15 to 20 minutes.
• Rinse vegetables quickly with cold water. Drain vegetables well. Blot dry with paper towels.
• Using a sharp knife, finely chop shallot and reserve for use in Savoury Aïoli (recipe follows).
• Spread a thin layer of Savoury Aïoli onto 8 bread slices. On aïoli side of 4 bread slices, layer on each ¼ cup spinach, 1 cheese slice, and 4 roast beef slices, folding and ruffling to fit. Place pickled courgette crosswise over roast beef. Top with pickled beetroot and a remaining bread slice, aïoli side down, to make 4 whole sandwiches.

- Using a serrated bread knife in a gentle sawing motion, trim and discard crusts from sandwiches. Cut each sandwich into 3 rectangles. Serve immediately, or cover with damp paper towels, place in a covered container, refrigerate, and serve within a few hours.

*If yellow courgette is not available, green courgette (zucchini) may be substituted.

Savoury Aïoli
Makes approximately ⅓ cup

Mayonnaise, English mustard, shallot, sherry vinegar, and turmeric combine to create this flavorful condiment for our Garden Vegetable, Roast Beef & Cheddar Tea Sandwiches.

⅓ cup mayonnaise
½ teaspoon prepared English mustard
½ teaspoon very finely chopped pickled shallot*
¼ teaspoon granulated sugar
¼ teaspoon sherry vinegar
⅛ teaspoon fine sea salt
⅛ teaspoon ground black pepper
⅛ teaspoon ground turmeric

- In a small bowl, stir together mayonnaise, mustard, shallot, sugar, vinegar, salt, pepper, and turmeric. Store in a covered container in the refrigerator and let flavors meld for up to a day before using.

*Reserved from preceding Garden Vegetable, Roast Beef & Cheddar Tea Sandwiches recipe.

Baked Ham & Cheese Sliders
Makes 12

Hawaiian rolls filled with layers of mustard, smoked ham, and Colby-Jack cheese offer a warm tea sandwich with the perfect balance of savory and sweet, which is the perfect accompaniment for Tomato-Basil Soup (page 20).

1 (12-ounce) package Hawaiian sweet rolls (12 rolls)
¼ cup plus 1 teaspoon yellow mustard, divided
8 thin slices deli-style smoked ham
1 cup coarsely shredded Colby-Jack cheese
3 tablespoons unsalted butter, melted
1 teaspoon firmly packed light brown sugar
½ teaspoon Worcestershire sauce
½ teaspoon sesame seeds

- Preheat oven to 350°. Lightly grease an 11x7-inch baking dish.
- Using a long, serrated bread knife in a gentle sawing motion, cut rolls in half horizontally as one whole piece. Place bottom half in baking dish. Spread 2 tablespoons mustard onto bottom half of rolls in baking dish. Lay ham slices evenly over mustard. Scatter cheese evenly over ham.
- Spread 2 tablespoons mustard onto cut surface of remaining top half of rolls. Place top half of rolls, mustard side down, over cheese.
- In a small bowl, stir together butter, remaining 1 teaspoon mustard, brown sugar, and Worcestershire sauce. Brush evenly over tops of rolls. Sprinkle tops of rolls evenly with sesame seeds.
- Bake until cheese melts and rolls are browned, 15 to 20 minutes. (If rolls are browning too quickly, loosely cover rolls with foil.) Using a sharp knife, cut into 12 individual sandwiches and cut each sandwich in half diagonally. Serve warm.

MAKE-AHEAD TIP: Rolls can be assembled in a baking dish, wrapped securely with plastic wrap, and stored in the refrigerator for up to a day in advance. Just before baking, brush with butter mixture.

- Using a serrated bread knife in a gentle sawing motion, trim and discard crusts from sandwiches. Cut each sandwich into 3 equal rectangles, creating 9 finger sandwiches. Cut each finger sandwich in half crosswise, creating 18 tea sandwiches. Serve immediately, or cover with damp paper towels, place in a covered container, and refrigerate for a few hours. For best flavor, let come to room temperature before serving.
- Just before serving, garnish each tea sandwich with a celery leaf, if desired.

Cranberry-Walnut Ham Salad Tea Sandwiches
Makes 16

Classic ham salad is embellished for autumn with the addition of dried cranberries and toasted walnuts for extra taste and texture. These delightful tea sandwiches are pictured with Watercress Pesto & Steak Crostini (page 99).

1½ cups finely chopped ham
½ cup sweetened dried cranberries, chopped
⅓ cup finely chopped celery
¼ cup finely chopped toasted walnuts
½ cup mayonnaise
1 tablespoon plus 1 teaspoon whole-grain mustard
1 teaspoon fresh lemon juice
¼ teaspoon seasoned salt
16 thin-cut slices whole grain bread

- In a medium bowl, stir together ham, cranberries, celery, and walnuts.
- In a separate bowl, whisk together mayonnaise, mustard, lemon juice, and salt. Add to ham mixture, stirring well to combine. Spread ¼ cup ham mixture onto 8 bread slices. Top each with a remaining bread slice to make 8 whole sandwiches.
- Using a serrated bread knife in a gentle sawing motion, trim and discard crusts from sandwiches. Cut each sandwich diagonally into 2 equal triangles. Serve immediately, or cover with damp paper towels, place in a covered container, refrigerate, and serve within a few hours.

MAKE-AHEAD TIP: Ham salad can be made up to 3 days in advance, covered tightly, and refrigerated until needed.

Creamy Celery & Blue Cheese Triple-Stack Sandwiches
Makes 18

Cream cheese studded with blue cheese, fresh celery, toasted almonds, fennel seeds, and lemon zest is a terrific filling for our triple-stack sandwiches, which are shown with Honeydew, Coppa & Feta Canapes (page 112).

1 (8-ounce) package cream cheese, softened
2 tablespoons fresh lemon zest
1 teaspoon fresh lemon juice
¼ teaspoon crushed fennel seeds
¼ teaspoon ground black pepper
3 tablespoons blue cheese crumbles
¼ cup finely chopped celery
2 tablespoons finely chopped toasted unblanched almonds
9 thin slices multigrain bread
Garnish: fresh celery leaves

- In a medium bowl, beat together cream cheese, lemon zest, lemon juice, fennel seeds, and pepper with a mixer at high speed until combined and creamy. Beat in blue cheese crumbles at medium-high speed until incorporated. Stir in celery and almonds.
- Spread an even layer of cheese mixture onto 6 bread slices. Stack bread slices in pairs, cheese sides up. Top each with a remaining plain bread slice, creating 3 triple-stack sandwiches.

Apple, Hazelnut & Cacao Nib Triple-Stack Tea Sandwiches
Makes 12

Striking a wonderful harmony of savory and sweet, as well as creamy and crunchy, these enticing tea sandwiches truly incorporate chocolate in an unexpected way with cacao nibs, which are the crushed or crumbled bits of cacao beans. They are shown here with Pork & Mole Crostini (page 98).

1 (8-ounce) package cream cheese, softened
1 teaspoon heavy whipping cream
½ teaspoon honey
¼ teaspoon fine sea salt
⅛ teaspoon ground black pepper
½ cup finely chopped green apple with peel
3 tablespoons cacao nibs
3 tablespoons coarsely chopped toasted blanched hazelnuts
2 tablespoons finely chopped celery
1 teaspoon everything bagel seasoning
12 slices very thin wheat bread

• In a medium bowl, beat together cream cheese, whipping cream, honey, salt, and pepper with a mixer at medium-high speed until well combined. Using a spoon, stir in apple, cacao nibs, hazelnuts, celery, and seasoning until well incorporated.
• Spread cream cheese mixture onto a bread slice. Top with another bread slice, and spread with cream cheese mixture. Top with a third bread slice to make a triple-stack sandwich. Repeat with remaining bread slices and cream cheese mixture to make a total of 4 whole sandwiches.
• Using a serrated bread knife in a gentle sawing motion, trim and discard crusts from sandwiches. Cut each sandwich into 3 equal rectangles. Serve immediately, or cover with damp paper towels, place in a covered container, refrigerate, and serve within 2 hours.

Pastrami-Avocado Tea Sandwiches
Makes 8

Pastrami gets a summertime makeover in this tea sandwich, bursting with fresh elements, such as tomato slices, arugula, and a creamy and tangy avocado spread. Serve alone or with Chicken Cordon Bleu Pastry Swirls (page 45) and Champagne & Tarragon Radish Flower Canapés (page 107) as pictured here.

8 slices firm white sandwich bread, frozen
4 slices deli-style pastrami
8 slices Campari-style tomato
Avocado-Lemon Spread (recipe follows)
1 cup coarsely chopped baby arugula
8 wooden picks

- Using a 2-inch round cutter, cut 16 rounds from frozen bread slices, discarding scraps. To prevent bread from drying out during assembly, cover with damp paper towels, or store in a resealable plastic bag, and let thaw at room temperature.
- In a large nonstick sauté pan, toast bread rounds over medium-high heat until light golden brown on both sides, approximately 2 to 3 minutes.
- Using a large sharp knife, cut pastrami slices in half lengthwise.
- Blot tomato slices with paper towels to remove excess juice.
- Spread a layer of Avocado-Lemon Spread onto toasted bread rounds. On spread side of 8 bread rounds, layer arugula, a tomato slice, and a pastrami piece, folding to fit. Top with a bread round, spread side down. Secure with a wooden pick. Serve immediately.

Avocado-Lemon Spread
Makes ½ cup

This delightfully nutritious spread—made from mashed avocado mixed with a little mayonnaise and seasoned with lemon juice, salt, and pepper—is the perfect replacement for plain mayonnaise on almost any tea sandwich.

1 Hass avocado, peeled and pitted
1 tablespoon mayonnaise
1 tablespoon fresh lemon juice, divided
¼ teaspoon fine sea salt
⅛ teaspoon ground black pepper

- In a small bowl and using a large fork, coarsely mash avocado. Add mayonnaise, 2 teaspoons lemon juice, salt, and pepper, stirring and mashing until combined and creamy. Pack mixture into a container and sprinkle top of mixture with remaining 1 teaspoon lemon juice. Cover surface of mixture with a sheet of plastic wrap, cover container, and refrigerate for a few hours until needed.

Darjeeling-Poached Chicken Salad Sandwiches

Makes 10

Classic chicken salad sandwiches are given a tasty teatime twist by adding Second Flush Darjeeling tea leaves to the filling.

3 quarts water
2 pounds boneless skinless chicken breasts
¾ cup loose Second Flush Darjeeling black tea leaves*
3 teaspoons fine sea salt, divided
1 cup mayonnaise
2 tablespoons chopped fresh parsley
1 teaspoon fresh lemon juice
½ cup chopped celery
½ cup quartered red grapes
¼ cup diced red onion
1 tablespoon thinly sliced fresh chives
¼ teaspoon ground black pepper
10 thin slices whole wheat bread, frozen

- In a large stockpot, bring 3 quarts water to a simmer over medium heat. Reduce heat to medium-low. Add chicken, tea leaves, and 2 teaspoons salt; cover and simmer until a meat thermometer inserted in thickest portion of chicken registers 165°, approximately 10 minutes. Remove chicken from liquid, and let cool completely. Strain tea leaves from liquid.
- Using a sharp knife, chop and reserve 2 tablespoons steeped tea leaves.
- In a large bowl, whisk together mayonnaise, parsley, 2 tablespoons reserved steeped tea leaves, and lemon juice.
- Using a sharp knife, finely chop chicken. Stir into mayonnaise mixture. Stir in celery, grapes, onion, chives, pepper, and remaining 1 teaspoon salt. Cover, refrigerate, and serve within a day.
- Spread a thick layer of chicken salad onto 5 frozen bread slices. Top each with a remaining frozen bread slices to make 5 whole sandwiches.
- Using a serrated bread knife in a gentle sawing motion, trim and discard crusts from sandwiches. Cut each sandwich diagonally into 2 triangles. Cover with damp paper towels, and let bread thaw completely (approximately 30 minutes) before serving, or cover with damp paper towels, place in a covered container, refrigerate, and serve within 2 hours.

"Flush" refers to the plant's new growth. If Second Flush tea is not available, another flush may be substituted.

Chicken Cordon Bleu Salad on Croissants

Makes 6

Mouthwatering sandwiches boast a tasty salad inspired by the iconic dish Chicken Cordon Bleu—roasted chicken, smoked ham, Dijon mustard, and Swiss cheese.

3 cups chopped roasted chicken
¾ cup chopped smoked ham
½ cup mayonnaise
⅓ cup chopped celery
¼ cup country-style Dijon mustard
2 tablespoons chopped fresh parsley
¼ teaspoon fine sea salt
¼ teaspoon ground black pepper
6 small croissants
6 slices baby Swiss cheese
6 pieces green leaf lettuce

- In a large bowl, stir together chicken, ham, mayonnaise, celery, mustard, parsley, salt, and pepper.
- Using a serrated bread knife in a gentle sawing motion, cut croissants in half lengthwise horizontally. Place a cheese slice on bottom half of each croissant. Top each with a lettuce leaf. Spoon chicken salad onto each lettuce layer, and top with remaining croissant halves to make 6 sandwiches. Serve immediately.

MAKE-AHEAD TIP: Chicken salad can be made a day in advance, covered, and refrigerated until needed.

Chicken & Artichoke Salad Tea Sandwiches
Makes 16

Tried-and-true chicken salad sandwiches are upgraded with the wonderful inclusion of marinated artichokes and fresh dill. Utilizing the meat from a rotisserie chicken for the filling is a time-saver.

½ cup mayonnaise
1 teaspoon fresh lemon zest
1 tablespoon fresh lemon juice
1 teaspoon fresh lime zest
1 tablespoon fresh lime juice
½ teaspoon fine sea salt
⅛ teaspoon ground black pepper
3 cups chopped rotisserie chicken
½ cup chopped marinated artichokes
1 tablespoon chopped fresh dill
8 slices wheat bread

• In a small bowl, stir together mayonnaise, lemon zest, lemon juice, lime zest, lime juice, salt, and pepper.
• In a large bowl, stir together chicken, artichokes, and dill. Add mayonnaise mixture to chicken mixture, stirring until chicken is uniformly moist. Cover, and refrigerate until cold, approximately 4 hours.
• Spread chicken salad in an even layer onto 4 bread slices. Top each with a remaining bread slice to make 4 whole sandwiches.
• Using a serrated bread knife in a gentle sawing motion, trim and discard crusts from sandwiches. Cut each sandwich into 4 equal rectangles, creating 16 tea sandwiches. Serve immediately, or cover with damp paper towels, place in a covered container, refrigerate, and serve within 4 hours.

Smoked Salmon & Pickled Okra Roll-Ups

Makes 12

These colorful roll-ups—made by placing smoked salmon, pickled okra, and cream cheese inside spinach tortillas— are quite easy to prepare and provide a lovely savory for afternoon tea and beyond. They are pictured with Chicken & Artichoke Salad Tea Sandwiches (opposite page) and Cucumber-Radish Canapés (page 112).

18 pickled okra spears
½ cup spreadable cream cheese, divided
2 (9-inch) spinach tortillas or wraps
8 ounces thinly sliced smoked salmon

• Cut ends and tips from okra spears. Blot okra dry with paper towels.
• Spread 2 tablespoons cream cheese onto each tortilla. Arrange an even layer of salmon slices over cream cheese layer of each tortilla. Spread 2 tablespoons remaining cream cheese over salmon layer of each tortilla.
• Starting at end of tortilla closest to you and referring to step-by-step photos, arrange 3 okra spears end to end to make a line (Photo 1). Make another line of okra spears end to end next to the first line (Photo 2). Place another 3 spears on top of initial line of okra (Photo 3). Roll up tortilla away from you, pressing firmly to keep okra spears together (Photo 4). Place rolled up tortilla seam side down. Repeat with remaining tortilla and okra.
• Using a serrated knife in a gentle, sawing motion, cut off ends of each roll to make a neat cylinder approximately 6 inches long.* Just before serving, cut each cylinder into 6 slices. Serve immediately.

*At this point, cylinders can be wrapped tightly with plastic wrap and stored in a covered container in the refrigerator for a few hours. When ready to serve, unwrap and continue with remaining recipe directions.

1

2

3

4

Lobster Salad Tea Sandwiches

Makes 12

A luxurious mixture of lobster, mayonnaise, lemon juice, fresh tarragon, and Campari tomatoes creates the filling for these coastal tea sandwiches.

4 (3-ounce) lobster tails
3 tablespoons mayonnaise
1 teaspoon fresh lemon juice
½ teaspoon chopped fresh tarragon
⅛ teaspoon fine sea salt
8 very thin slices white bread, frozen
12 pieces green leaf lettuce
12 slices Campari tomato
Garnish: yellow grape tomato slices

• Place lobster tails in a steamer basket set over a large saucepan containing boiling water. (Do not let water touch steamer basket). Cover saucepan, and return to a boil. Steam until tails are pink and meat is opaque white, 5 to 7 minutes. Remove tails and let cool. Pick meat from tails. Chop lobster meat.
• In a small bowl, stir together lobster meat, mayonnaise, lemon juice, tarragon, and salt. Cover bowl, and refrigerate until cold, approximately 4 hours.
• Using a 1½-inch round cutter, cut 24 rounds from frozen bread slices, discarding scraps. To prevent bread from drying out during assembly, cover bread rounds with damp paper towels, and let thaw for 15 minutes.
• Place lettuce on each of 12 bread rounds, and then top with a Campari tomato slice. Top each with lobster salad and a remaining bread round to create 12 sandwiches.
• Garnish with a yellow grape tomato slice, if desired, and secure with a frilled pick. Serve immediately.

Roast Beef–Radish Tea Sandwiches

Makes 12

These attractive tea sandwiches are lovely year-round and boast layers of roast beef, watercress, radish, and homemade Sour Cream–Horseradish Aïoli on potato bread.

12 slices potato sandwich bread, frozen
Sour Cream–Horseradish Aïoli (recipe follows)
½ cup watercress leaves
12 slices ultra-thin deli-style roast beef
Garnish: ¼ cup paper-thin radish slices and watercress sprigs

• Using a 2-inch square cutter, cut 24 shapes from frozen bread slices. Let bread squares thaw in a resealable plastic bag or covered with damp paper towels.
• Spread a layer of Sour Cream–Horseradish Aïoli onto 12 bread squares. Arrange several watercress leaves on aïoli side of bread squares. Fold roast beef slices in half, and ruffle to fit bread squares. Top each with a remaining bread square, aïoli side down, to create 12 sandwiches. Serve immediately, or cover with damp paper towels, place in a covered container, refrigerate, and serve within 2 hours.
• Just before serving, garnish each sandwich with 5 overlapping radish slices and a sprig of watercress.

Sour Cream–Horseradish Aïoli

Makes ⅓ cup

Mayonnaise, sour cream, horseradish, salt, and pepper combine to create this creamy and piquant spread for our Roast Beef–Radish Tea Sandwiches.

⅓ cup mayonnaise
1 tablespoon sour cream
½ teaspoon prepared horseradish
1 pinch fine sea salt
1 pinch ground black pepper

• In a small bowl, stir together mayonnaise, sour cream, horseradish, salt, and pepper. Cover, refrigerate, and use within a day.

CURRIED EGG SALAD
CANAPÉS
page 97

DELECTABLE

Canapés & Crostini

THESE DAINTY AND DELICIOUS MORSELS
ARE PERFECT FOR AN ELEGANT TEA PARTY
OR A FESTIVE OCCASION.

Strawberry & Goat Cheese Crostini
Makes 16

These brilliantly light, bite-size morsels are made of toasted baguette slices that are topped with a heavenly layer of a honeyed goat cheese spread and crowned with chopped strawberries and chopped fresh tarragon. Crunchy, creamy, and refreshing, these pretty canapés will become your go-to recipe for seasonal parties. They are pictured with Curried Shrimp & Mango Salad Tea Sandwiches (page 67) and Ham & Pineapple Pinwheels (page 67).

16 (¼-inch-thick) baguette slices
1 tablespoon olive oil
4 ounces goat cheese, softened
2 ounces cream cheese, softened
1 tablespoon honey
½ teaspoon fine sea salt
¼ teaspoon ground white pepper
½ cup fresh strawberries, stemmed and chopped into ½-inch pieces
Garnish: chopped fresh tarragon

- Preheat oven to 375°. Line a rimmed baking sheet with foil.
- Brush bread slices with a layer of olive oil. Place prepared bread slices, oil side up, on prepared baking sheet.
- Bake until very lightly golden, approximately 5 minutes; increase oven temperature to broil. Broil until golden, approximately 1½ to 2 minutes more, watching carefully. Let cool. Store crostini in a resealable plastic bag or in an airtight container and use within a day.
- In the work bowl of a food processor*, pulse together cheeses until combined, scraping down sides of bowl as needed. Add honey, salt, and pepper. Process until light and fluffy.
- Spread approximately 2 teaspoons goat cheese mixture onto each crostino. Top each crostino with 1 teaspoon strawberries.
- Garnish with tarragon, if desired. Serve immediately.

*If a food processor isn't available, use a mixer.

Omelet & Asparagus Canapés
Makes 9

Miniature omelet roulades, which encase asparagus spears, are sliced and placed on thin round crackers to make dainty and delicious savory bites for springtime.

6 to 9 thin asparagus spears
1 tablespoon salted butter
3 large eggs
2 tablespoons heavy whipping cream
⅛ teaspoon fine sea salt
2 teaspoons snipped fresh dill
Lemon-Dill Aïoli (recipe follows)
Thin round crackers
Garnish: fresh dill sprigs

• In a saucepan large enough to accommodate asparagus spears, bring 2 inches of water to a boil over high heat.
• Trim and discard tough ends from asparagus. Add asparagus spears to boiling water, and cook just until fork tender, 1 to 2 minutes. Plunge asparagus into ice water to stop the cooking process. Pat asparagus dry with paper towels.
• In a medium nonstick sauté pan, melt butter over medium heat.
• In a medium bowl, whisk together eggs, cream, and salt until frothy. Add to sauté pan, and sprinkle with snipped dill. Let eggs cook, lifting edges with a spatula to let egg run underneath cooked edges. When omelet is firm enough to lift, flip and cook on the other side just until set.
• Slide omelet onto a cutting board. Starting at end of omelet closest to you, place a row of asparagus spears. Make another row of asparagus next to the first one. Place a third row of asparagus on top of the first two. Roll up omelet away from you into a cylinder. Let cool. Cut in ½-inch slices.
• Spread a small amount of Lemon-Dill Aïoli onto a cracker, and top with an omelet slice. Repeat with remaining omelet slices, crackers, and aïoli.
• Garnish each with a dill sprig, if desired. Serve within an hour.

We used Rutherford & Meyer Gourmet Wafers.

Lemon-Dill Aïoli
Makes ¼ cup

Mayonnaise, fresh dill, lemon, salt, and pepper meld together in this fantastically light spread for our Omelet & Asparagus Canapés.

¼ cup mayonnaise
1½ teaspoons snipped fresh dill
¼ teaspoon fresh lemon zest
1 teaspoon fresh lemon juice
⅛ teaspoon fine sea salt
⅛ teaspoon ground black pepper

• In a small bowl, stir together mayonnaise, dill, lemon zest, lemon juice, salt, and pepper. Cover, refrigerate, and use within a day.

baller, scoop a well into each cucumber slice. Blot cucumber slices dry with paper towels.
• Place approximately ¼ teaspoon crème fraîche mixture into each well.
• Cut salmon into ½-inch-wide strips of varying lengths. Starting on the outer edge of cucumber wells, arrange salmon strips in concentric circles to resemble a rose until filled. Serve immediately, or cover lightly with plastic wrap and store in the refrigerator for up to an hour.
• Just before serving, garnish centers of salmon roses with lemon zest, if desired.

MAKE-AHEAD TIP: Crème fraîche mixture can be made a day in advance, stored in a covered container, and refrigerated. Cucumber sections can be prepared a day in advance, wrapped in plastic, stored in a resealable plastic bag, and refrigerated.

Salmon Roses on Cucumber Rounds
Makes 8

Strips of smoked salmon shaped into rosettes and placed into the wells of scooped-out cucumber slices make for a light, yet eye-catching, savory that really stands out when served alongside traditional tea sandwiches. A simple crème fraîche spread adds pleasing flavor to these gluten-free canapés, which are pictured with Egg & Cress Tea Sandwiches (page 78) and Garden Vegetable, Roast Beef & Cheddar Tea Sandwiches (page 78).

3 tablespoons crème fraîche
2 teaspoons fresh lemon zest
⅛ teaspoon fine sea salt
⅛ teaspoon ground black pepper
½ English cucumber
1 (4-ounce) package smoked salmon slices
Garnish: fresh lemon zest

• In a small bowl, whisk together crème fraîche, lemon zest, salt, and pepper. Cover bowl and refrigerate for several hours for flavors to meld.
• Using a Y-shaped vegetable peeler, scrape cucumber vertically, creating alternate stripes. Using a sharp knife, cut 8 (½-inch) round slices from cucumber, discarding excess or reserving for another use. Using a mini melon

Crab Cake Crostini
Makes 21

Toasted baguette slices (crostini) host appetizing crab cakes crowned with roasted red pepper and a lovely rémoulade for an elegant savory that will warm hearts and satisfy palates for afternoon tea. They are pictured, opposite page, with Creole Filet Tea Sandwiches (page 72) and Beet Hummus Frico Cups (page 123).

1 long, thin French baguette
3 tablespoons extra-virgin olive oil
1 (8-ounce) container pasteurized fresh lump crabmeat, picked free of shell
1 cup panko (Japanese breadcrumbs), divided
1 large egg
1½ tablespoons minced roasted red pepper
1 tablespoon minced green onion, green parts only
1 tablespoon mayonnaise
1 tablespoon fresh lemon juice
¼ teaspoon fine sea salt
⅛ teaspoon ground black pepper
½ cup vegetable oil or avocado oil
Lemon-Chive Rémoulade (recipe follows)
21 (1-inch-long) chive pieces
21 roasted red pepper hearts*

- Preheat oven to 350°. Line a rimmed baking sheet with parchment paper.
- Using a serrated bread knife in a sawing motion, cut 21 (¼-inch) crosswise slices from baguette. Place bread slices on prepared baking sheet. Using a pastry brush, brush top side of bread slices lightly with olive oil.
- Bake until crisp, 7 to 10 minutes. Let crostini cool completely, store in an airtight container, and use the same day.
- In a medium bowl, stir together crabmeat, ¼ cup panko crumbs, egg, roasted red pepper, green onion, mayonnaise, lemon juice, salt, and black pepper, stirring well. Using a levered 2-teaspoon scoop, drop portions of crab mixture into remaining ¾ cup bread crumbs, pressing crumbs onto crab cakes to cover completely. Place breaded crab cakes in an airtight container and refrigerate for at least 30 minutes and up to 3 hours.
- In a large sauté pan, heat vegetable oil or avocado oil over medium-high heat. Fry crab cakes until golden brown, 2 to 3 minutes per side. Drain on paper towels.
- To assemble crostini, spread Lemon-Chive Rémoulade onto each crostino. Top each with a crab cake and a small dollop of rémoulade. Top each with a chive piece placed diagonally and a red pepper heart, pressing down lightly to adhere to crab cake with rémoulade. Serve immediately.

*Place drained whole roasted red peppers on a cutting surface. Using a very small (¾-inch) Linzer-type heart-shaped cutter, cut 21 hearts from peppers. Store in a covered container with brine from jar until needed. Blot well on paper towels before using as a garnish.

Lemon-Chive Rémoulade
Makes ½ cup

This rémoulade, a traditional French sauce, is imparted with lemon and fresh chives to make a sumptuous spread to mingle with crab in our enticing crostini.

½ cup mayonnaise
1½ teaspoons fresh lemon zest
2 teaspoons fresh lemon juice
2 teaspoons minced fresh chives
⅛ teaspoon ground black pepper

- In a small bowl, stir together mayonnaise, lemon zest, lemon juice, chives, and pepper. Cover, refrigerate, and use within a day.

Prosciutto & Artichoke Herbed Crostini
Makes 12

Layers of prosciutto, artichoke hearts, and tomato sit atop a crispy crostino (toasted baguette slice) spread with a vibrant herb-laced aïoli. Because prosciutto is dry-cured with salt, it can be safely consumed uncooked, as we have used it in this recipe. However, if preferred, prosciutto can be cooked in a skillet until crisp instead.

12 (½-inch) slices baguette bread*
1 tablespoon extra-virgin olive oil
Herbed Aïoli (recipe follows)
12 very thin slices prosciutto
⅓ cup chopped canned artichoke hearts
⅓ cup chopped fresh tomato
Garnish: olive oil and basil leaves

- Preheat oven to 350°. Line a rimmed baking sheet with parchment paper.
- Brush bread slices with a layer of olive oil. Place prepared bread slices, oil side up, on prepared baking sheet.
- Bake until very light golden brown, 5 to 7 minutes. Let cool. Store crostini in a resealable plastic bag or in an airtight container.
- Spread a thin layer of Herbed Aïoli onto oil side of each crostino. Place a prosciutto slice on each crostino, folding and ruffling prosciutto to fit. Top prosciutto with artichoke and tomato.
- Garnish each crostino with a drizzle of oil and a basil leaf, if desired. Serve immediately.

*Using a serrated bread knife in a gentle sawing motion, cut ½-inch-thick bread slices at a diagonal from a long skinny baguette.

Herbed Aïoli
Makes approximately ⅓ cup

Three fresh herbs, lemon juice, and red wine vinegar transform basic mayonnaise into a flavor-packed aïoli.

⅓ cup mayonnaise
1 tablespoon finely chopped fresh basil
1 teaspoon finely chopped fresh oregano
1 teaspoon fresh lemon juice
1 teaspoon finely chopped flat-leaf parsley
½ teaspoon red wine vinegar
¼ teaspoon fine sea salt
⅛ teaspoon ground black pepper

- In a small bowl, stir together mayonnaise, basil, oregano, lemon juice, parsley, vinegar, salt, and pepper until combined. Store in a small covered container, refrigerate, and use within 2 days.

Curried Egg Salad Canapés
Makes 24

A crunchy cracker replaces traditional sandwich bread as the base for the curried egg salad in this tasty savory.

6 large eggs, hard-cooked, peeled, and chopped*
⅓ cup mayonnaise
2 teaspoons yellow mustard
½ teaspoon dry English mustard powder
½ teaspoon curry powder
¼ teaspoon fine sea salt
⅛ teaspoon ground black pepper
1/16 teaspoon ground turmeric
1 English cucumber
2 tablespoons Major Grey's mango chutney
24 large round crackers**
1 tablespoon finely chopped red bell pepper
1 tablespoon finely chopped green onion tops

- In a medium bowl, stir together eggs, mayonnaise, yellow mustard, mustard powder, curry powder, salt, pepper, and turmeric. Place in a covered container and refrigerate to allow flavors to meld, 4 hours or overnight.
- Using a mandoline or a sharp paring knife, cut 48 very thin slices from cucumber. Lay cucumber slices on paper towels and blot dry.
- Brush or spread a very thin layer of mango chutney onto crackers. Arrange 2 cucumber slices in an overlapping fashion atop chutney layer on each cracker. Using a 1-tablespoon levered scoop, place a mound of egg salad atop cucumber layer. Top egg salad evenly with bell pepper and green onion. Serve immediately.

*For a quick-and-easy way to chop eggs into uniform pieces, press hard-cooked eggs through a gridded wire cooling rack set over a bowl.
**We used Carr's Table Water Crackers.

Pork & Mole Crostini
Makes 12

Slices of pork tenderloin and a lovely fresh salad consisting of avocado, cotija cheese, and corn kernels sit atop a satisfyingly crunchy toasted baguette slice that is smothered with a light layer of mole (pronounced MOH-leh) sauce, a traditional Mexican mixture of dried chili peppers and cacao. Crostini are pictured with Apple, Hazelnut & Cacao Nib Triple-Stack Tea Sandwiches (page 82) and Beef-Mushroom Carbonnade in Pastry Shells (page 46).

1 (1.25-pound) pork tenderloin
¼ teaspoon garlic salt
¼ teaspoon ground paprika
⅛ teaspoon ground black pepper
1 tablespoon plus 2 teaspoons extra-virgin olive oil, divided
12 (½-inch-thick) slices baguette bread
2 tablespoons mole concentrate*
½ cup chicken broth, plus extra for thinning
½ cup small-diced avocado
2 teaspoons fresh lime juice
½ cup cooked fresh corn kernels
½ cup cotija cheese crumbles

- Preheat oven to 350°. Line a rimmed baking sheet with foil. Line another rimmed baking sheet with parchment paper.
- Place pork on foil-lined baking sheet. Season pork evenly with garlic salt, paprika, and pepper. Drizzle with 2 teaspoons olive oil and rub oil and seasonings into meat.
- Roast in oven until desired degree of doneness is achieved (145° on an instant-read meat thermometer for medium-rare), 25 to 30 minutes. Wrap foil around pork to cover and let pork rest for at least 10 minutes.** Using a sharp knife, cut pork into ½-inch slices.
- Place baguette slices on parchment-lined baking sheet. Using a pastry brush, brush baguette slices with remaining 1 tablespoon oil.
- Bake until lightly golden and crisp, approximately 10 minutes. Let crostini cool completely. (For best freshness, store in an airtight container and use the same day.)
- In a small saucepan, heat together mole concentrate and chicken broth over medium heat, stirring constantly until concentrate dissolves into chicken broth. Simmer sauce over low heat for 3 to 4 minutes,stirring frequently. Add enough chicken broth to achieve desired spreadable consistency.

- Just before serving, in a small bowl, toss avocado with lime juice.
- Spread a thin layer of mole sauce onto crostini. Trimming pork to fit, if needed, top each crostino with a pork slice. Spoon a small amount of mole sauce on top of pork. Top with avocado, corn, and cheese. Serve immediately.

*We used Doña María Mole Mexican Sauce.
**At this point, pork can be wrapped well and stored in the refrigerator for up to a day.

Watercress Pesto & Steak Crostini
Makes 18

Tender slivers of steak and a tasty layer of Watercress Pesto sit atop toasted baguette slices to create a delicious savory for teatime and beyond, pictured with Cranberry-Walnut Ham Salad Tea Sandwiches (page 80).

18 (¼-inch-thick) slices baguette
3 tablespoons extra-virgin olive oil, divided
1 (4- to 5-ounce) beef tenderloin filet
½ teaspoon fine sea salt
½ teaspoon ground black pepper
Watercress Pesto (recipe follows)
Garnish: shaved Parmesan cheese* and fresh basil

- Preheat oven to 400°.
- Place baguette slices in a single layer on rimmed baking sheet. Brush slices with 2 tablespoons olive oil.
- Bake until golden brown, 8 to 10 minutes, turning halfway through baking time. Let crostini cool on a wire rack. (For best freshness, store in an airtight container and use the same day.)
- Pat steak with paper towels to dry. Season all sides with salt and pepper. Let steak sit at room temperature for 30 minutes.
- In a small nonstick skillet, heat remaining 1 tablespoon oil over medium-high heat. Cook steak until desired doneness, 3 to 4 minutes per side, reducing heat to medium, if necessary. Place steak on cutting board and let rest for 15 minutes before slicing. Cut steak in half. Slice each section against the grain into 9 thin slices.
- Spread a thin layer of Watercress Pesto onto crostini. Top each with a steak slice.
- Garnish with cheese and basil, if desired. Serve immediately.

*We used a vegetable peeler to shave Parmesan cheese.

Watercress Pesto
Makes ½ cup

This bright and herbaceous spread, made with pecans rather than pine nuts, is perfect for our Steak Crostini and is equally great on tea sandwiches, pizza, and more.

2 tablespoons finely chopped toasted pecans
2 tablespoons coarsely grated Parmesan cheese
1 small to medium clove garlic
2 cups loosely packed watercress
½ cup loosely packed basil leaves
3 tablespoons extra-virgin olive oil
¼ teaspoon fine sea salt

- In the work bowl of a food processor, pulse together pecans, cheese, and garlic until mixture resembles coarse crumbs. Add herbs, pulsing to combine. With food processor running, slowly add olive oil to bring pesto together, scraping down sides of work bowl as needed. Add salt, pulsing to combine.

MAKE-AHEAD TIP: *Pesto can be made up to 3 days in advance, stored in an airtight container, and refrigerated until needed.*

CANAPÉS & CROSTINI | *Teatime Savories*

Seared Scallop & Chorizo Canapés with Herb Sauce
Makes 12

A seared scallop topped with a homemade herb sauce of cilantro, parsley, garlic, and oregano sits atop a slice of Spanish-style chorizo for a tasty, breadless canapé. This unique morsel is equal parts spicy and buttery, with delectable flavor reigning supreme.

½ cup packed fresh cilantro leaves
¼ cup packed fresh parsley leaves
1 tablespoon sherry vinegar
½ teaspoon grated fresh garlic
½ teaspoon dried oregano
¾ teaspoon fine sea salt, divided
¼ teaspoon ground cumin
⅛ teaspoon red pepper flakes
3 tablespoons extra-virgin olive oil, divided
12 medium-large sea scallops, tendons removed
¼ teaspoon ground black pepper
12 (⅛-inch) slices dry Spanish-style chorizo

- In the container of a blender, process together cilantro, parsley, vinegar, garlic, oregano, ¼ teaspoon salt, cumin, and pepper flakes until herbs are coarsely chopped and ingredients are well combined, stopping to scrape down sides of container with a rubber spatula. With blender running, gradually add 2 tablespoons olive oil in a steady stream until mixture is finely chopped but not smooth. Transfer herb mixture to an airtight container, refrigerate, and use within a day.
- Place scallops between several thick layers of paper towels, gently pressing to absorb moisture. Let sit at room temperature for 15 minutes.
- In a nonstick 12-inch skillet, heat remaining 1 tablespoon oil over medium-high heat.
- Sprinkle both sides of scallops with pepper and remaining ½ teaspoon salt. Add to hot skillet and sear until golden brown, 2 to 3 minutes per side. Transfer to a plate, cover loosely with foil, and use within an hour.
- On a serving platter, arrange chorizo slices in a single layer. Top each chorizo slice with a scallop. Top each scallop with ¼ teaspoon herb mixture. Serve immediately.

Fish Taquitos with Creamy Slaw
Makes 24

Petite, afternoon-tea–size tacos—filled with tender cod and a flavorful slaw (thanks to agave nectar, lime juice, sour cream, and coriander)—are a fantastic addition to the savories course of a coastal tea menu.

24 (6-inch) corn tortillas
1¼ teaspoons fine sea salt, divided
2 tablespoons plus 2 teaspoons fresh lime juice, divided
2 tablespoons extra-virgin olive oil
2 teaspoons agave nectar, divided
1 teaspoon chili powder
½ teaspoon paprika
½ teaspoon ground coriander, divided
¼ teaspoon ground cumin
1 (8-ounce) skinless cod fillet
1 tablespoon sour cream
½ cup shredded slaw mix
1 tablespoon chopped fresh cilantro
1 tablespoon sliced green onions
¼ teaspoon ground black pepper
Garnish: lime wedges

- Preheat oven to 350°. Spray an upside-down 24-well mini muffin pan with cooking spray. Line a rimmed baking sheet with foil.
- Using a 2¾-inch round cutter, cut 24 rounds from tortillas. Wrap tortilla rounds in damp paper towels and place on a microwave-safe plate. Microwave tortillas on high until pliable, 15 to 30 seconds. Working quickly while tortilla rounds are soft, spray both sides of each tortilla round with cooking spray and sprinkle with ½ teaspoon salt. Shape each tortilla into a taco shell and place between upside-down wells of prepared muffin pan. (If a tortilla won't stay open, loosely roll up and spray a small piece of foil with cooking spray, and place it inside tortilla.)
- Bake until shells are crisp and hold their shape, 10 to 12 minutes. Let cool completely before removing taco shells from muffin pan.
- In a resealable plastic bag, combine 2 tablespoons lime juice, olive oil, 1 teaspoon agave nectar, chili powder,

paprika, ¼ teaspoon coriander, and cumin. Add fish fillet to marinade in bag, seal bag, and gently work marinade into fish. Let marinate at room temperature for 15 minutes.
• In a medium bowl, stir together sour cream, ¼ teaspoon salt, remaining 2 teaspoons lime juice, remaining 1 teaspoon agave nectar, and remaining ¼ teaspoon coriander. Add slaw mix, cilantro, and onions, stirring to coat. Cover and refrigerate until ready to use.
• Place oven rack 4 to 6 inches away from heating element. Turn oven on broil.
• Remove fish from marinade and pat dry with paper towels. Sprinkle with pepper and remaining ½ teaspoon salt. Place fish on prepared baking sheet.
• Broil fish until it flakes easily with a fork, 5 to 7 minutes.
• To assemble taquitos, divide fish evenly among taco shells. Top each with 1 teaspoon slaw. Serve immediately with lime wedges, if desired.

MAKE-AHEAD TIPS: Taco shells can be prepared a day in advance and stored in an airtight container. Slaw can be prepared a day in advance, covered, and refrigerated until needed. For best texture, prepare fish and assemble taquitos just before serving.

Smoked Salmon & Caper Cream Cheese–Filled Cucumber Canapés
Makes 16

Hollowed-out thick slices of cucumber are pretty and oh-so tasty when piped with a piquant cream cheese filling of smoked salmon, capers, mint, and lemon zest. They are pictured here with Honey Ham & Dijon Tea Sandwiches (page 76).

1 (8-ounce) package cream cheese, softened
1 (3-ounce) package smoked salmon
1 tablespoon balsamic capers, drained
1 tablespoon chopped fresh mint
1 teaspoon fresh lemon zest
⅛ teaspoon ground white pepper
⅛ teaspoon garlic powder
2 English cucumbers
Garnish: fresh mint leaves

- In the work bowl of a food processor, pulse together cream cheese, salmon, capers, mint, lemon zest, pepper, and garlic powder until combined and smooth. Transfer mixture to an airtight container, and refrigerate until very cold and flavors meld, 6 to 8 hours.
- Trim and discard ends from cucumbers. Cut 16 (½-inch-thick) sections from cucumbers, making sure cuts are straight so cucumber sections sit level. Turn each section onto a cut side, and place on a work surface. Using a melon baller, scoop a shallow cavity from each cucumber section, discarding center pulp.
- Transfer cold cream cheese mixture to a piping bag fitted with large star tip (Wilton #1M or Ateco #825). Pipe mixture into cavity of each cucumber section.
- Garnish each canapé with a mint leaf. Serve immediately.

MAKE-AHEAD TIP: Cucumber sections can be prepared earlier in the day, placed in an airtight container, and refrigerated. Blot dry with paper towels, if needed, just before using.

Salmon Rillettes
Makes 12

Our take on rillettes (meat slow-cooked in fat and stored in more fat) features fresh salmon poached in seasoned water and then mixed with chopped smoked salmon, melted butter, and heavy cream to achieve the unctuous texture of the traditional spread. Fresh herbs, lemon, and capers—not to mention the radish and watercress garnish—give these savory morsels a bright taste.

½ cup water
1 slice lemon
½ shallot, sliced
1 bay leaf
2 sprigs fresh dill
3 ounces skinless fresh salmon fillet
2 ounces smoked salmon, finely chopped
2 tablespoons unsalted butter, melted
1½ tablespoons heavy whipping cream
1 tablespoon finely chopped fresh dill
1 tablespoon finely chopped fresh chives
½ tablespoon fresh lemon zest
½ tablespoon fresh lemon juice
1 teaspoon finely chopped capers
¼ teaspoon Worcestershire sauce
⅛ teaspoon ground black pepper
12 (½-inch-thick) slices French bread, frozen
1 tablespoon salted butter, softened
Garnish: thin radish slices and watercress

• In a medium saucepan, combine ½ cup water, lemon slice, shallot, bay leaf, and dill sprigs. Add salmon fillet to pan. Bring water to a gentle boil. Adjust heat to bring water to a simmer, cover pan, and cook salmon for 1 minute. Remove pan from heat and let salmon sit in water to poach, approximately 20 minutes. Transfer salmon from poaching liquid to a clean surface. Using a fork, finely flake salmon.
• In a medium bowl, stir together flaked salmon, smoked salmon, butter, cream, dill, chives, lemon zest, lemon juice, capers, Worcestershire sauce, and pepper until combined. Pack salmon salad into a resealable glass jar or bowl, cover, and refrigerate until flavors meld, several hours and up to a day.
• Preheat oven to 400°. Line a rimmed baking sheet with parchment paper.
• Using a 2-inch round cutter, cut 12 rounds from frozen bread, discarding scraps. Spread a layer of softened

butter onto bread rounds and place in a single layer on prepared baking sheet, butter side up.
• Bake until bread is lightly golden and crisp, 7 to 9 minutes.
• Spread a thick layer of salmon salad onto bread rounds.
• Garnish each canapé with a radish slice and a watercress sprig, if desired. Serve immediately.

KITCHEN TIP: To create thick, even layers of salmon salad, place bread round inside the 2-inch round cutter, top bread round with salmon salad, pressing with a spoon to spread salmon salad to edges. Remove cutter. Repeat with remaining bread rounds and salmon salad.

Smoked Fish Toasts
Makes 12

Smoked fish—whether mackerel or trout—horseradish, fresh chives, and other additions elevate cheese toast from warm comfort food to teatime delight, especially when paired with a cup of strong black tea.

6 to 12 thick slices white bread
1 cup flaked smoked trout or mackerel fillets
¾ cup freshly grated Parmesan cheese, divided
¼ cup heavy whipping cream
1 tablespoon mayonnaise
1 tablespoon chopped fresh chives
2 teaspoons prepared horseradish
¼ teaspoon ground black pepper
Garnish: minced chives and cracked black pepper

• Preheat oven to 400°. Line a rimmed baking sheet with parchment paper.
• Using a serrated bread knife in a gentle sawing motion, cut 12 (4x2-inch) rectangles from bread slices. Arrange bread rectangles in a single layer on prepared baking sheet.
• In a medium bowl, stir together fish, ½ cup cheese, cream, mayonnaise, chives, horseradish, and pepper. Spread 1 tablespoon fish mixture onto each bread rectangle.
• Bake until fish mixture begins to brown and bread is toasted, 7 to 9 minutes. Sprinkle with remaining ¼ cup cheese. Serve warm or at room temperature within an hour.
• Just before serving, garnish with minced chives and cracked black pepper, if desired.

Cucumber-Tarragon Fleur-de-Lis Canapés
Makes 8

Cucumber sandwiches are staples for the savory course of afternoon tea. This iteration, spread with an herbaceous, crème fraîche aïoli, is presented as a canapé with a tarragon garnish to resemble a fleur-de-lis and is pictured, opposite page, with Duck Salad Brioche Sandwiches (page 60) and Salmon Rillettes (page 103).

4 thin slices multigrain bread, frozen
¼ cup crème fraîche
2 tablespoons mayonnaise
1 teaspoon fresh lemon zest
1 teaspoon finely chopped fresh tarragon
½ teaspoon very finely grated sweet onion
¼ teaspoon fine sea salt
1/16 teaspoon ground black pepper
½ English cucumber
Garnish: fresh tarragon sprigs

• Using a 1½-inch square cutter, cut 8 squares from bread slices, discarding scraps. Cover bread squares with damp paper towels to prevent drying out, and let thaw at room temperature.
• In a small bowl, stir together crème fraîche, mayonnaise, lemon zest, tarragon, onion, salt, and pepper until combined.
• Using a sharp knife, cut cucumber in half lengthwise. Using a mandoline, cut very thin lengthwise slices from cucumber halves. (Blot dry on paper towels, if necessary.)
• Spread a layer of crème fraîche mixture onto bread squares. Arrange 4 cucumber slices in a shingled, parallel fashion over crème fraîche mixture side of each bread square, trimming cucumber slices to fit bread squares. Serve immediately, or cover with damp paper towels, place in a covered container, and refrigerate for up to an hour before serving.
• Just before serving, garnish each canapé with a tarragon sprig, if desired, shaping sprig to resemble a fleur-de-lis.

MAKE-AHEAD TIPS: Bread squares can be cut out a day in advance and stored in a resealable plastic bag to prevent drying out. Crème fraîche mixture can be made up to a day in advance, stored in a covered container, and refrigerated to allow flavors to meld.

Lemon-Lime Scallop Canapés
Makes 12

Tender sea scallops are placed atop English water crackers and a bed of watercress that has been lightly tossed with a homemade Lemon-Lime Vinaigrette to produce a phenomenal and sophisticated bite.

12 large sea scallops
¼ teaspoon fine sea salt
⅛ teaspoon ground black pepper
3 tablespoons olive oil
1 tablespoon salted butter
2 cups chopped watercress
Lemon-Lime Vinaigrette (recipe follows)
12 English water crackers
Garnish: fresh lemon zest and fresh lime zest

• Blot scallops dry on paper towels. Season with salt and pepper.
• In a large sauté pan, heat olive oil over medium-high heat. When oil begins to shimmer, add scallops, and let sit for exactly 1 minute. Reduce heat to medium, turn scallops over, and let sit for 1 minute. Remove from heat, and add butter. Let butter melt, stirring to coat scallops in melted butter. Remove scallops from pan, and set aside.
• Toss watercress with just enough Lemon-Lime Vinaigrette to lightly dress. Divide watercress evenly among crackers. Top each cracker with a scallop. Lightly drizzle scallops with remaining vinaigrette.
• Garnish each canapé with lemon zest and lime zest, if desired. Serve immediately.

Lemon-Lime Vinaigrette
Makes ½ cup

¼ cup extra-virgin olive oil
2 tablespoons fresh lemon juice
2 tablespoons fresh lime juice
½ teaspoon granulated sugar
¼ teaspoon fine sea salt
⅛ teaspoon ground black pepper

• In a jar with a screw-top lid, combine olive oil, juices, sugar, salt, and pepper. Shake vigorously until emulsified.

MAKE-AHEAD TIP: Lemon-Lime Vinaigrette can be made a day in advance, placed in a covered container, and refrigerated until needed. Let come to room temperature before using, and shake well.

Champagne & Tarragon Radish Flower Canapés
Makes 8

Almost too pretty to eat, these charming canapés feature the boldly harmonious tastes of radish and tarragon perfectly balanced by unctuous cream cheese. A mandoline on the thinnest setting possible is key to getting radish slices that are even and pliable enough to fold without breaking. These pretty canapés are pictured with Chicken Cordon Bleu Pastry Swirls (page 45) and Pastrami-Avocado Tea Sandwiches (page 83).

4 slices firm white sandwich bread, frozen
4 ounces cream cheese, softened
1 teaspoon finely chopped fresh tarragon
¾ teaspoon Champagne vinegar
⅛ teaspoon fine sea salt
⅛ teaspoon ground black pepper
6 large radishes
Garnish: tarragon leaves and ground pink peppercorns

- Using a 1¾-inch fluted round cutter, cut 8 rounds from frozen bread slices, discarding scraps. To prevent bread from drying out during assembly, cover with damp paper towels, or store in a resealable plastic bag, and let thaw at room temperature.
- In a small bowl, stir together cream cheese, tarragon, vinegar, salt, and pepper until creamy. Transfer mixture to a piping bag fitted with a large star tip (Wilton #1). Pipe upright dollops of cream cheese mixture onto thawed bread rounds.
- Trim root ends from radishes and discard ends. Using a mandoline* or a sharp paring knife, cut very thin crosswise slices from radishes. (Slices must be thin enough to bend without breaking**. For best results, radish slices should be approximately the same diameter and are best taken from widest sections of radishes.) Fold each slice in half and then into quarters without creasing slices. Place 5 or 6 folded radish slices on top of each bread round, arranging to resemble a flower. Gently press flower into cheese mixture to adhere. Serve immediately, or place in a container, lightly covered with damp paper towels, and refrigerate for up to an hour.
- Just before serving, garnish with tarragon leaves and ground pink peppercorns, if desired.

*We had best results with a Kyocera Advanced Ceramic Adjustable Mandoline.
**If radishes are not pliable, sprinkle them with a pinch of salt and let stand until they become soft enough to fold, approximately 15 minutes, if necessary. Pat dry before using."

1

2

3

4

Lemon-Dill Aïoli
Makes ⅓ cup

Mayonnaise, dill, lemon, and a bit of salt and pepper meld together in this light and herb-forward spread.

⅓ cup mayonnaise
1 tablespoon snipped fresh dill
½ teaspoon fresh lemon zest
1 teaspoon fresh lemon juice
⅛ teaspoon fine sea salt
⅛ teaspoon ground black pepper

- In a small bowl, stir together mayonnaise, dill, lemon zest and juice, salt, and pepper until combined. Use immediately, or cover and refrigerate for several hours until needed.

Smoked Salmon Blini
Makes approximately 28

Toothsome and fluffy petite pancakes, also known as blini, are topped with a luscious layer of Creamy Horseradish-Dill Sauce and crowned with a thin slice of smoked salmon to produce a delightfully appetizing and visually interesting savory to pair with a cup of hot tea. They are pictured, opposite page, with Date & Roasted Chicken Salad Tea Sandwiches (page 66) and Caramelized Leek & Pancetta Quiche (page 33).

1 cup all-purpose flour
1 teaspoon baking powder
½ teaspoon fine sea salt
¼ teaspoon granulated sugar
¼ teaspoon ground black pepper
¾ cup whole milk
1 large egg
1 tablespoon unsalted butter, melted
½ teaspoon Worcestershire sauce
¼ teaspoon cayenne pepper sauce*
3 tablespoons finely chopped green onion (green parts only)
1 tablespoon canola oil or avocado oil
Creamy Horseradish-Dill Sauce (recipe follows)
1 (4-ounce) package thinly sliced smoked salmon
Garnish: fresh dill sprigs

Asparagus & Ham Tartines
Makes 12

Slices of French baguette are layered with smoked ham, asparagus spears, and Lemon-Dill Aïoli in this fantastic bite paired with Soupe à l'Oignon (page 18).

6 asparagus spears
12 (½-inch-thick) slices French baguette
Lemon-Dill Aïoli (recipe follows)
12 thin slices smoked deli ham
Garnish: fresh dill sprigs

- Preheat oven to 400°. Line a rimmed baking sheet with parchment paper.
- Snap off and discard tough ends from asparagus spears. Arrange asparagus on prepared baking sheet.
- Bake until asparagus is tender when pierced with the tip of a sharp knife, 5 to 7 minutes. Let cool completely. Cut spears in half vertically and then into ½-inch pieces.
- Reduce oven temperature to 350°. Line another rimmed baking sheet with parchment paper.
- Place baguette slices on prepared baking sheet.
- Toast until baguette slices (crostini) are very lightly golden brown and crisp, 5 to 7 minutes. Let crostini cool completely, store in an airtight container, and use the same day.
- Just before serving, spread Lemon-Dill Aïoli onto crostini. Ruffle ham slices to fit crostini. Arrange asparagus pieces, cut side down, on top of ham.
- Garnish with dill sprigs, if desired. Serve immediately.

108 Teatime Savories | CANAPÉS & CROSTINI

- In a medium bowl, whisk together flour, baking powder, salt, sugar, and pepper.
- In another medium bowl, whisk together milk, egg, butter, Worcestershire sauce, and pepper sauce until well blended. Whisk in green onion. Add to flour mixture, whisking until just combined. (A few lumps are OK, so don't overbeat.)
- Line a tray or rimmed baking sheet with paper towels.
- Brush a nonstick griddle lightly with oil, and heat over medium-high heat. Using a 1-tablespoon measuring spoon, drop batter in scant 1-tablespoon portions, 1-inch apart, onto hot griddle. Batter should spread into a fairly round shape. (If batter is too thick, add a little more milk.) Cook until bubbles appear in tops of pancakes and edges look dry. Using a turner, flip pancakes; cook until browned. If pancakes are browning too much, reduce heat. Let pancakes cool completely on prepared tray, and use within 2 hours.
- To assemble blini, spread desired amount of Creamy Horseradish-Dill Sauce onto cooled pancakes. Divide small pieces of smoked salmon among pancakes.
- Garnish with fresh dill, if desired. Serve immediately.

*We used Tabasco.

Creamy Horseradish-Dill Sauce

Makes approximately ½ cup

This slightly spicy, piquant, and herbaceous condiment provides a bright boost of flavor for our Smoked Salmon Blini. This tasty spread would also be wonderful on tea sandwiches and for recipes that utilize beef.

½ cup sour cream
2 tablespoons mayonnaise
1 tablespoon prepared creamy horseradish
1 tablespoon minced fresh dill
2 teaspoons fresh lemon zest
⅛ teaspoon fine sea salt
⅛ teaspoon ground black pepper

- In a medium bowl, stir together sour cream, mayonnaise, horseradish, dill, lemon zest, salt, and pepper to combine. Use immediately, or cover, refrigerate, and use within a day.

Beanie Flatbread Hummus Bites
Makes 12

Homemade hummus is piped onto crunchy flatbread beanie shapes and topped with slivers of carrot and celery to present a cute and healthy savory that hat lovers will adore, pictured with Turkey-Swiss Roulades (page 65).

1 (9x7½-inch) rectangle multigrain flatbread
2 tablespoons plus 2 teaspoons extra-virgin olive oil
1 (15.5-ounce) can chickpeas, drained
½ cup roasted red peppers, drained
½ teaspoon fresh lemon zest
2 tablespoons fresh lemon juice
½ teaspoon fine sea salt
2 tablespoons tahini
1 tablespoon water
12 (1½x⅛-inch) pieces matchstick-cut carrot
12 (1½x⅛-inch) pieces matchstick-cut celery

• Preheat oven to 350°. Line a rimmed baking sheet with parchment paper.
• Using a 2½-inch beanie-shaped cutter, cut 12 shapes from flatbread, discarding scraps. Arrange beanie shapes on prepared baking sheet. Using a pastry brush, brush shapes with 2 teaspoons olive oil.
• Bake until crisp, 5 to 7 minutes. Let cool completely on baking sheet.
• In the work bowl of a food processor, pulse together chickpeas, peppers, lemon zest and juice, salt, and remaining 2 tablespoons oil until smooth. With processor running, add tahini and 1 tablespoon water, processing until smooth.
• Transfer hummus to a piping bag fitted with a small star tip (Wilton #21). Pipe a small dollop at the top of chips for a pompom. Pipe 2 lines of hummus at the base of chips for the beanie cuff. Place a carrot stick and a celery stick on top of each upper hummus line, trimming sticks to fit, if necessary. Serve immediately.

MAKE-AHEAD TIP: Chips and hummus can be made the day before. Store chips in an airtight container at room temperature, and store hummus in an airtight container in the refrigerator. Assemble beanies just before serving.

Tarragon & Cucumber Flower Canapés
Makes 16

These beautiful and frilly canapés feature a billowing cucumber flower top to create a picturesque bite for afternoon tea. They are pictured here with Petite Savory Éclairs (page 125).

3.5 ounces (approximately 7 tablespoons) salted European-style butter, room temperature
1 tablespoon finely chopped fresh tarragon
1 teaspoon white wine vinegar
1 teaspoon finely chopped fresh parsley
1 teaspoon fresh lemon zest
⅛ teaspoon ground black pepper
8 slices firm white sandwich bread, frozen
64 paper-thin slices English cucumber with peel
Garnish: fresh lemon zest

• In a small bowl, stir together butter, tarragon, vinegar, parsley, lemon zest, and pepper until well blended.
• Using a 1¾-inch square cutter, cut 16 squares from frozen bread, discarding scraps.
• Spread a thin layer of butter mixture onto each bread square. Fold each cucumber slice in half and then in quarters. Pinch the inner fold of each cucumber slice between thumb and forefinger, and place on bread square, green edges up. Repeat 3 times per canapé. Arrange folds to resemble a flower.
• Garnish cucumber flowers with lemon zest in centers, if desired. Cover with damp paper towels, and let bread thaw completely, approximately 30 minutes. Serve immediately.

Cucumber-Radish Canapés
Makes 12

A mayonnaise mixture laden with chives, lemon, and a hint of shallot secures shingled slices of cucumber and radish to dainty bread rectangles. These simple, yet appetizing, canapés are incredibly revitalizing for a summertime tea and are pictured here with Chicken & Artichoke Salad Tea Sandwiches (page 86) and Smoked Salmon & Pickled Okra Roll-Ups (page 87).

⅓ cup mayonnaise
1 teaspoon finely chopped fresh chives
1 teaspoon fresh lemon juice
½ teaspoon minced shallot
⅛ teaspoon fine sea salt
⅛ teaspoon ground black pepper
4 slices white sandwich bread, frozen
1 English cucumber
1 cup whole radishes*

• In a small bowl, stir together mayonnaise, chives, lemon juice, shallot, salt, and pepper.
• Using a serrated bread knife in a gentle sawing motion, trim and discard crusts from frozen bread. Cut each bread slice into 3 even rectangles that are the same width as cucumber. Place bread rectangles in a resealable plastic bag to let thaw.
• Using a mandoline on the thinnest setting, cut 36 (⅛-inch) slices from cucumber and 24 (⅛-inch) slices from radishes.
• Spread a layer of mayonnaise mixture onto each bread rectangle. On mayonnaise side of each bread rectangle, alternately shingle 3 cucumber slices and 2 radish slices, beginning and ending with cucumber. Serve immediately, or cover with damp paper towels, place in a covered container, refrigerate, and serve within 2 hours.

*Select radishes that are close to the same diameter as the cucumber.

Honeydew, Coppa & Feta Canapés
Makes 12

Similar to prosciutto, coppa, also known as capocollo, is an Italian cold cut made by dry-curing pork shoulder. Serve atop crunchy crostini layered with honeydew melon and feta cheese for a marvelous salty-sweet bite. Because preserved lemon can be a somewhat potent flavor experience, we recommend exercising restraint with it, but do use it, as it adds welcome citrus notes. The canapé is pictured with Lemony Couscous-Shrimp Salad (page 122) and Creamy Celery & Blue Cheese Triple-Stack Sandwiches (page 80).

12 (½-inch) slices baguette bread
1 tablespoon extra-virgin olive oil
12 thin slices coppa
12 thin slices honeydew melon*
12 thin slices feta cheese*
½ tablespoon minced preserved lemon
Garnish: microgreens

• Preheat oven to 350°. Line a rimmed baking sheet with parchment paper.
• Brush bread slices with a layer of olive oil. Place prepared bread slices, oil side up, on prepared baking sheet.
• Bake until very light golden brown, approximately 5 minutes. Let cool. Store crostini in a resealable plastic bag or in an airtight container and use the same day.
• Fold each coppa slice into quarters. Place a folded coppa piece on oil side of each crostino, trimming to fit if necessary. Place a melon slice and a cheese slice over coppa. Sprinkle with a few pieces of minced preserved lemon.
• Garnish with microgreens, if desired. Serve immediately.

*Slices should be approximately the same size as the baguette slices.

Cucumber-Watercress Canapés
Makes 12

Teatime guests will be most impressed by the seemingly complex arrangement of the cucumber slices on these canapés, but you don't have to divulge just how truly simple overlapping the cucumber slice halves actually is. They are shown at right with Roast Lamb Salad Tea Sandwiches with Pistachio-Mint Pesto (page 69).

6 slices firm white sandwich bread, frozen
1 English cucumber
⅓ cup mayonnaise
⅓ cup packed watercress leaves, finely chopped
1 teaspoon fresh lemon zest
½ teaspoon fresh lemon juice
⅛ teaspoon fine sea salt
⅛ teaspoon ground black pepper
Garnish: watercress sprigs

- Using a 2-inch round cutter, cut 12 rounds from frozen bread slices, discarding scraps. Cover bread rounds with damp paper towels to prevent drying out while letting thaw.
- Using a small hand-held mandoline or a sharp knife, cut 48 thin, uniform round slices from cucumber. Lay slices in a single layer on paper towels to absorb excess moisture.
- In a small bowl, stir together mayonnaise, watercress, lemon zest, lemon juice, salt, and pepper until combined to make an aïoli. Spread aïoli in an even layer onto bread rounds.
- Stack 2 cucumber slices together. Using a sharp knife, cut stacked slices in half to form half moons. Repeat with 2 more cucumber slices.
- Referring to how-to photos, on a bread round, place 1 stack of halved cucumber slices on top of aïoli (Photo 1). Place another stack of halved slices at a 90-degree overlapping angle to the first stack (Photo 2).

Place a third stack at a 90-degree overlapping angle to the second stack (Photo 3). Place the fourth stack at a 90-degree overlapping angle to the third stack and underlapping the first stack (Photo 4).
- Garnish with a watercress sprig, if desired.

MAKE-AHEAD TIP: Aïoli can be made up to a day in advance, stored in an airtight container, and refrigerated to allow flavors to meld. Canapés can be made up to an hour before serving, covered with damp paper towels, placed in an airtight container, and refrigerated.

1

2

3

4

Cucumber Canapés with Dilled Butter
Makes 15

A homemade dilled butter elevates this classic and refreshing cucumber canapé to a new level.

4 tablespoons salted butter, softened
2 teaspoons snipped fresh dill
¼ teaspoon fresh lemon zest
4 slices firm white sandwich bread, frozen
15 (⅛-inch-thick) slices English cucumber
Garnish: fresh dill sprigs

- In a small bowl, stir together butter, snipped dill, and lemon zest.
- Using a 1½-inch round cutter, cut 15 shapes from frozen bread, discarding scraps. Place bread rounds in a resealable plastic bag, or cover with damp paper towels until thawed.
- Using an offset spatula, spread a layer of dilled butter onto each bread round. Top each with a cucumber slice. Serve immediately, or cover with damp paper towels, place in a covered container, refrigerate, and serve within 2 hours.
- Just before serving, garnish each cucumber slice with a fresh dill sprig, if desired.

Salmon Petits Toasts
Makes 15

Featuring marvelous texture and taste, these petite salmon toast points, pictured opposite page, are simple to prepare, but be sure to allow at least 4 hours to refrigerate the topping so its flavors can meld.

4 ounces smoked salmon
4 ounces cream cheese, softened
2 tablespoons sour cream
1 teaspoon freshly ground horseradish root
⅛ teaspoon ground white pepper
15 petits toasts*

• In the work bowl of a food processor, combine salmon, cream cheese, sour cream, horseradish root, and white pepper. Pulse until well blended and smooth. Transfer mixture to a covered container, and refrigerate until cold, at least 4 hours.
• Just before serving, let mixture soften briefly at room temperature for ease of piping. Transfer mixture to a piping bag fitted with a large open-star tip (Wilton #1M), and pipe onto toasts in an upright fashion. Serve immediately.

*We used Trois Petits Cochons.

Smoked Salmon–Cucumber Canapés with Niçoise Olive Tapenade
Makes 6

Hollowed out English cucumbers are filled with thin slices of smoked salmon and a homemade Niçoise Olive Tapenade to produce a refined bite for a lovely afternoon tea.

1 English cucumber
Niçoise Olive Tapenade (recipe follows)
6 thin slices smoked salmon
Garnish: fresh parsley and lemon peel curls

• Trim ends from cucumber. Using a channel knife, cut vertical stripes on cucumber. Cut 6 (1¼-inch) sections from cucumber. Using a melon baller, scoop out a well in each section and discard.

• Divide Niçoise Olive Tapenade among cucumber sections. Place a rolled smoked salmon piece in each section, nestling to fit and ruffling to form a flower shape.
• Garnish each with a parsley leaf and a lemon peel curl, if desired.

Niçoise Olive Tapenade
Makes ⅔ cup

This tasty French condiment adds briny flavor to our Smoked Salmon–Cucumber Canapés.

⅓ cup pitted Niçoise olives
⅓ cup pitted bright green olives
1 tablespoon chopped fresh parsley
1 tablespoon chopped fresh basil
1 teaspoon capers
1 teaspoon fresh lemon zest
1 teaspoon fresh lemon juice
¼ teaspoon chopped fresh garlic
1 tablespoon extra-virgin olive oil

• In the work bowl of a food processor, combine olives, parsley, basil, capers, lemon zest, lemon juice, and garlic, pulsing until mixture is finely chopped and well blended. Transfer mixture to a covered container, refrigerate, and use within a day.
• Just before using, stir in olive oil.

PORK & SHRIMP LUMPIA
page 127

BEEF SALTEÑAS
page 126

MISCELLANEOUS

Savories Galore

INTERNATIONAL HORS D'OEUVRES, SEAFOOD CREATIONS, AND LIGHT BITES WILL UNDOUBTEDLY IMPRESS GUESTS FOR AFTERNOON TEA.

Shrimp-Topped Avocado & Cucumber Microgreen Salads

Makes 8 (3-ounce) servings

Served in cordial glasses, these refreshing petite salads feature a bottom layer of flavorful avocado purée and subsequent layers of diced cucumber and microgreens topped with cooked shrimp and dressed in a tangy White Wine Vinaigrette. They are so good that the only complaint you'll get is that the servings are simply too small.

2 cups water
1 lemon slice
1 bay leaf
1 (6-inch) rib celery, coarsely chopped
8 medium/large shrimp with tails, peeled and deveined
2½ cups coarsely chopped ripe avocado
2 teaspoons fresh lemon juice
¼ teaspoon fine sea salt
⅛ teaspoon ground black pepper
1 cup finely diced English cucumber
White Wine Vinaigrette (recipe follows), divided
1 cup microgreens

- In a small saucepan over high heat, bring to a boil together 2 cups water, lemon slice, bay leaf, and celery. Boil for 3 minutes to flavor poaching water. Remove pan from heat and add shrimp. Cover pan and let sit until shrimp are poached, approximately 5 minutes. Transfer shrimp to a large bowl, and cover with ice to stop cooking. Let cool completely. Remove shrimp and blot dry on paper towels.
- In a medium bowl, using a fork, mash together avocado, lemon juice, salt, and pepper until a smooth purée forms. Transfer avocado purée to a piping bag with the tip cut off.
- Pipe avocado purée evenly into 8 (3-ounce) clear cordial glasses. Using the tip of a spoon, smooth avocado purée in an even layer. Top avocado layer with cucumber. Drizzle cucumber with a little White Wine Vinaigrette. Divide microgreens among glasses. Drizzle with more vinaigrette.
- Dip shrimp into remaining vinaigrette, letting excess drip off, and place shrimp atop microgreens layer. Serve immediately, or refrigerate and serve within 2 hours.

MAKE-AHEAD TIP: *Shrimp can be poached a day in advance, stored in a covered container, and refrigerated. Avocado purée can be made a few hours in advance and placed in a small bowl. Drizzle surface of purée with lemon juice, press plastic* wrap onto surface, completely covering surface, and refrigerate. If surface of avocado purée has browned, scrape away and discard browned portion. Remaining purée will be good to use.

White Wine Vinaigrette
Makes ⅔ cup

Bright white wine vinegar combined with shallot, fresh dill, lemon juice, and sugar creates a vibrant vinaigrette that is perfect for almost any salad but especially for our Shrimp-Topped Avocado & Cucumber Microgreen Salads.

⅓ cup extra-virgin olive oil
¼ cup white wine vinegar
2 tablespoons fresh lemon juice
1 teaspoon very finely chopped shallot
1 teaspoon very finely chopped fresh dill
½ teaspoon granulated sugar
¼ teaspoon fine sea salt
⅛ teaspoon ground black pepper

- In a small glass jar with a screw-top lid, combine olive oil, vinegar, lemon juice, shallot, dill, sugar, salt, and pepper. Shake vigorously until combined and emulsified. Let sit at room temperature for 1 hour for flavors to meld.

MAKE-AHEAD TIP: *White Wine Vinaigrette can be made a day in advance and stored in the refrigerator. Let come to room temperature and shake again before using.*

Herbed Deviled Eggs
Makes 24

An herbaceous twist on classic deviled eggs, this recipe incorporates fresh chives and dill into the filling and as an alternating garnish to create a tastier and more elegant version of the beloved appetizer.

12 large eggs
1 teaspoon baking soda
⅔ cup mayonnaise
2 tablespoons sour cream
1 tablespoon chopped fresh chives
1 tablespoon chopped fresh dill
½ teaspoon fine sea salt
Garnish: fresh dill sprigs and minced fresh chives

- Place eggs in a large saucepan. Cover eggs with water by 3 inches. Add baking soda and bring to a boil over medium-high heat, boil for 2 minutes. Cover, and remove from heat. Let eggs rest for 8 to 9 minutes.
- Drain hot water from pan and rinse eggs in pan in cold water. Drain and peel eggs. Using a sharp knife, cut eggs in half lengthwise. Carefully remove yolks from whites and place yolks in a deep medium bowl. Reserve whites.
- In the same medium bowl, add mayonnaise and sour cream to yolks. Beat with a mixer at medium speed until smooth. Stir in chives, dill, and salt. Transfer yolk mixture into a piping bag fitted with a medium star tip (Ateco #869). Pipe yolk mixture into reserved egg whites. Place in a covered container and refrigerate until ready to serve.
- Just before serving, place on an egg plate and garnish yolk mixture with dill and chives, if desired.

Savory Lobster Cheesecakes
Makes 18

These decadent morsels put cheesecake in a savory light, with lobster, lemon, and fresh herbs mingling masterfully in the rich filling. A buttery cracker crust and a dollop of crème fraîche and black caviar on top complete the elegant bite.

42 buttery crackers*
½ cup salted butter, melted
2 (8-ounce) packages cream cheese, softened
1 tablespoon heavy whipping cream
¼ cup all-purpose flour
1 teaspoon fresh lemon zest
1 teaspoon fresh lemon juice
½ teaspoon hot pepper sauce
½ teaspoon fine sea salt
⅛ teaspoon ground black pepper
2 large eggs
8 ounces lobster tail meat
½ cup fresh corn kernels
3 tablespoons finely chopped red bell pepper
1 tablespoon finely chopped fresh chives
1 tablespoon finely chopped shallot
1 tablespoon finely chopped fresh parsley
Garnish: crème fraîche and black caviar

- Preheat oven to 350°.
- Lightly spray 18 wells of 2 (12-well) mini cheesecake pans with cooking spray.
- In the work bowl of a food processor, pulse crackers until very finely crumbled.
- In a medium bowl, combine crumbs and butter, stirring to blend. Divide crumb mixture evenly among prepared wells of pans, approximately 2 teaspoons crumb mixture per well. Press mixture firmly to form bottom crust.
- Bake until golden brown, approximately 6 minutes. Let cool completely.
- In a large bowl, combine cream cheese, whipping cream, flour, lemon zest, lemon juice, hot pepper sauce, salt, and black pepper. Beat at medium-high speed with a mixer until smooth and creamy. Add eggs, beating until just incorporated. Stir in lobster, corn, bell pepper, chives, shallot, and parsley. Divide mixture evenly among prepared wells of pans, approximately 3 tablespoons per well.
- Bake until cheesecakes are set and slightly puffed, approximately 12 minutes. Let cool completely in pans before removing.
- Garnish with crème fraîche and black caviar, if desired.

*We used Ritz crackers.

KITCHEN TIP: *For a pretty presentation, place crème fraîche in a piping bag fitted with a large open-star tip (Wilton #1M), and pipe rosettes onto cheesecakes.*

MAKE-AHEAD TIP: *Cheesecakes can be made a day in advance, wrapped in plastic wrap in pans, and refrigerated overnight. Just before serving, remove from pans, place on a rimmed baking sheet, and warm slightly in a 350° oven.*

Loaded Potato Twists
Makes 6

Skewers and a sharp paring knife are all you need to make the cuts on these mini spiral versions of Hasselback potatoes. Be sure to open the cuts by pulling each potato apart slightly along its skewer to allow the melted butter and spice mix to reach as many crevices as possible before baking. These petite spuds are pictured with Roast Beef Pastries (page 49) and Shrimp Salsa Cups (page 55).

6 (6- to 8-inch) skewers
6 baby Yukon gold potatoes*
1 teaspoon garlic powder
½ teaspoon fine sea salt
½ teaspoon ground black pepper
¼ teaspoon smoked paprika
¼ teaspoon cumin powder
3 tablespoons unsalted butter, melted
Garnish: sour cream, shredded Cheddar cheese, cooked bacon**, and finely chopped chives

- Preheat oven to 400°. Line a rimmed baking sheet with parchment paper.
- Insert a 6- to 8-inch skewer lengthwise all the way through the center of a potato. Using a sharp paring knife, make an angled slit at the very top of skewered potato. Keeping knife in place, carefully rotate potato around knife, making a continuous spiral cut all the way around potato. Pull spiral apart slightly and place on prepared baking sheet. Repeat with remaining potatoes and remaining skewers.
- In a small bowl, combine garlic powder, salt, pepper, paprika, and cumin.
- Using a pastry brush, brush potatoes with butter. Sprinkle with spice mixture, turning to coat evenly with spices.
- Bake potatoes until lightly browned and crispy, 25 to 30 minutes, rotating baking sheet halfway through baking. Carefully remove and discard skewers. Serve warm.
- Garnish with sour cream, cheese, bacon, and chives, if desired.

*We used Potatoes Inspirations Honey Gold Baby Potatoes. For best presentation, choose potatoes that are similarly sized and shaped.
**We finely chopped 4 thick-cut slices bacon; cooked bacon in a medium skillet over medium heat, stirring frequently, until browned and crisp; removed bacon using a slotted spoon; and let it drain and cool on paper towels before using.

MISCELLANEOUS SAVORIES | *Teatime Savories* **121**

Lemony Couscous-Shrimp Salad
Makes 12 servings

Hollowed-out lemon halves make perfect tea-size bowls for this refreshing salad.

6 small lemons
1 cup Shrimp Stock* (recipe follows)
16 medium shrimp, deveined in shells with tails (reserve shells for Shrimp Stock, if making)
¾ cup dried couscous
¼ teaspoon fine sea salt
1 tablespoon unsalted butter, softened
Lemon-Thyme Vinaigrette (recipe follows)
¼ cup finely chopped fresh tomato
¼ cup chopped finely chopped yellow bell pepper
1 tablespoon finely chopped flat-leaf parsley
1 tablespoon finely chopped buttery green olives**
1 tablespoon finely chopped fresh chives
Garnish: fresh mint leaves

- Using a serrated knife in a gentle sawing motion, cut lemons in half lengthwise.
- Using a small grapefruit spoon, scrape lemon to remove fruit pulp, creating 12 "lemon bowls." Using a serrated knife, cut a small piece from bottoms of lemon bowls so they will sit level.
- In a medium saucepan, bring Shrimp Stock to a boil. Add shrimp. Turn off heat, and cover pan with a lid. Let poach for 5 minutes. Reserving Shrimp Stock, use a slotted spoon to transfer shrimp from pan to a medium bowl, and cover with ice. Let sit for 2 to 3 minutes to stop shrimp from cooking. Remove shrimp and blot dry on paper towels. Using a sharp knife, finely chop shrimp.
- In a medium saucepan, bring reserved Shrimp Stock to a boil. Add dried couscous and salt. Turn off heat, cover pan with lid, and let sit for 5 minutes. Using a fork, stir in butter to combine and fluff couscous.
- Transfer couscous to a medium bowl. Stir in enough Lemon-Thyme Vinaigrette to moisten couscous. Let cool completely before stirring in chopped shrimp, tomato, bell pepper, parsley, olives, and chives.
- Fill lemon bowls with couscous mixture. Drizzle with additional vinaigrette, if desired.
- Garnish with fresh mint, if desired. Serve immediately.

Water or purchased seafood stock can be used instead of Shrimp Stock, if desired.
**We used Castelvetrano olives.*

MAKE-AHEAD TIP: *Hollowed-out lemon halves can be prepared up to a day in advance, wrapped in plastic wrap, placed in a resealable plastic bag, and refrigerated. Lemony Couscous-Shrimp Salad can be prepared up to a day in advance, stored in a covered container, and refrigerated.*

Shrimp Stock
Makes 1½ cups

A simple, homemade stock using the shells of the seafood from the Lemony Couscous-Shrimp Salad imparts tremendous flavor to the shrimp and the couscous. Although you can substitute water or store-bought seafood stock, why would you?

2 cups water
16 shrimp shells
1 rib celery, chopped
3 sprigs fresh thyme
½ teaspoon dried minced garlic
½ teaspoon dried minced onion
1 slice lemon

- In a medium saucepan, combine 2 cups water, shrimp shells, celery, thyme, garlic, and onion. Bring mixture to a boil over medium-high heat. Cover saucepan (tilt lid to prevent boiling over) and boil for 15 minutes. Remove pan from heat. Add lemon slice and close lid. Let sit for 15 minutes.
- Using a fine-mesh sieve, strain mixture into a medium bowl. Use immediately or let cool to room temperature, store in a covered container, refrigerate, and use within a day.

Lemon-Thyme Vinaigrette

Makes ½ cup

Bright with fresh citrus and fresh thyme, this tangy dressing is delightful on any salad but was created with our Lemony Couscous-Shrimp Salad in mind.

¼ cup fresh lemon juice
¼ cup extra-virgin olive oil
1½ teaspoons finely minced shallot
1 teaspoon coarse-ground Dijon mustard
½ teaspoon granulated sugar
½ teaspoon finely chopped fresh thyme leaves
¼ teaspoon fine sea salt
⅛ teaspoon ground black pepper

- In a small glass jar with a screw-top lid, combine lemon juice, olive oil, shallot, mustard, sugar, thyme, salt, and pepper. Shake vigorously to emulsify. Let sit at room temperature for 1 hour for flavors to meld. Shake again before using.

MAKE-AHEAD TIP: Lemon-Thyme Vinaigrette can be made up to a day in advance and refrigerated. Let come to room temperature before using. Shake to emulsify.

Beet Hummus Frico Cups

Makes 8

Wonderfully simple and unique for teatime, these petite frico cups feature a delicate Parmesan cheese vessel filled with a nutritious and vibrant purchased beet hummus. They will undoubtedly impress guests with their taste and appearance.

1 cup loosely packed finely grated Parmesan cheese*
½ cup prepared beet hummus**
⅓ cup loosely packed rainbow microgreens

- Preheat oven to 350°. Line a large, rimmed baking sheet with a silicone baking mat or parchment paper.
- Sprinkle cheese evenly into 8 circles (each approximately 3 inches across) onto prepared baking sheet.
- Bake until cheese melts and is very lightly browned, 6 to 8 minutes. Working quickly and using a thin-blade metal spatula, lift melted cheese circles from baking sheet and drape each over the back of a well of a mini muffin pan. Let cheese cool completely before carefully and gently removing and inverting frico cups. Store in a single layer in an airtight container and use the same day.
- Just before serving, using a levered 2-teaspoon scoop, portion hummus into each frico cup.
- Garnish with microgreens. Serve immediately.

*Make sure you use a block of Parmesan cheese and freshly grate it with a Microplane fine grater.
**We used Ithaca Lemon Beet Hummus.

Bannann Peze with Quick Pikliz
Makes approximately 8 servings

This tea-sized interpretation of a traditional Haitian dish features plantain chunks that are soaked in salted water, fried, flattened, soaked again, and fried again and then topped with a flavorful slaw.

4 cups water
2 tablespoons fine sea salt
1 large green plantain, peeled and cut crosswise into 1-inch slices
Vegetable oil, for frying
Quick Pikliz (recipe follows)

• In a medium bowl, stir together 4 cups water and salt until salt dissolves. Add plantain. Let stand for 15 minutes. Using a slotted spoon, transfer plantain to paper towels, reserving salted water.
• In a large skillet, pour oil to a depth of 1 inch. Heat over medium-high heat until a deep-fry thermometer registers 325°. Fry plantain in hot oil until lightly golden, 8 to 10 minutes. Let drain on paper towels.
• Using the bottom of a ramekin, flatten plantain slices to a ¼-inch thickness. Return plantain to salted water. Let stand for 5 minutes. Remove, drain on paper towels, and fry a second time until crisp, approximately 5 minutes. Let drain on paper towels.
• To serve, top each plantain slice with Quick Pikliz. Serve immediately.

Quick Pikliz
Makes 1½ cups

A tangy slaw scented with cloves and chilis, pikliz adds a perfect burst of acidity to Bannann Peze.

2½ cups green cabbage slaw mix
¼ cup white vinegar
2 tablespoons thinly sliced red bell pepper
2 tablespoons thinly sliced green bell pepper
2 tablespoons thinly sliced orange bell pepper
2 tablespoons thinly sliced shallot
½ teaspoon seeded and thinly sliced Thai chili pepper
½ teaspoon fine sea salt
2 whole cloves

• In a medium bowl, toss together slaw mix, vinegar, bell peppers, shallot, chili pepper, salt, and cloves. Cover and refrigerate for at least 1 hour or overnight. Just before serving, remove and discard cloves. Serve cold or at room temperature.

Petite Savory Éclairs
Makes 34

This savory version of the beloved French pastry boasts traditional choux dough filled with a delectable Herbed Goat Cheese and is pictured with Tarragon & Cucumber Flower Canapés (page 110).

¾ cup plus 1 tablespoon water, divided
¼ cup plus 2 tablespoons unsalted European-style butter, softened and cubed
2 teaspoons granulated sugar
¼ teaspoon fine sea salt
¾ cup all-purpose flour
3 large eggs, room temperature
1 large egg white
Herbed Goat Cheese (recipe follows)
Garnish: fleur de sel

- Preheat oven to 400°. Line 2 rimmed baking sheets with parchment paper or with silicone baking mats.
- In a medium saucepan, combine ¾ cup water, butter, sugar, and salt. Cook over medium heat until butter melts. Add flour, stirring vigorously with a wooden spoon. Cook, stirring constantly, until dough pulls away from sides of pan, 1 to 2 minutes. Remove from heat, and let stand for 2 minutes, stirring a few times to cool dough.
- Transfer dough to a large bowl. Add eggs, one at a time, beating with a mixer at medium speed until well incorporated. (Dough should be smooth and shiny.)
- Transfer dough to a piping bag fitted with a medium round tip (Wilton #12). Pipe 2½-inch-long pieces of dough onto prepared baking sheets. (If necessary, pat dough with damp fingers to refine shape.)
- In a small bowl, whisk together egg white and remaining 1 tablespoon water. Brush tops of éclairs with egg mixture. Sprinkle with fleur de sel, if desired.
- Bake for 15 minutes. Reduce oven temperature to 350°. Bake until éclairs are very golden brown, approximately 10 minutes more. (Insides will be dry.) Let cool completely. Using a sharp knife, make small slits in 2 places on bottom of each éclair.
- Place Herbed Goat Cheese in a piping bag fitted with a small open star tip (Wilton #18). Pipe cheese into éclairs through bottom slits. Serve immediately, or place in a covered container, refrigerate, and serve within 2 hours.

Herbed Goat Cheese
Makes 3 cups

Dill, chives, basil, parsley, and thyme meld together with goat cheese in this satisfying filling for our Petite Savory Éclairs. This spread would additionally be great on savory scones or as a sandwich filling.

8 ounces goat cheese, room temperature
8 ounces cream cheese, room temperature
⅔ cup heavy whipping cream
½ teaspoon granulated shallots*
¼ teaspoon fine sea salt
⅛ teaspoon ground black pepper
2 tablespoons finely chopped fresh dill
2 tablespoons finely chopped fresh chives
2 tablespoons finely chopped fresh basil
1 tablespoon finely chopped fresh flat-leaf parsley
1 teaspoon finely chopped fresh thyme

- In a medium bowl, beat together goat cheese, cream cheese, heavy cream, shallots, salt, and pepper with a mixer at high speed until combined. Add all herbs, beating at medium speed until incorporated. Use immediately, or place in a covered container, refrigerate, and use within a day.

*We used Penzeys Granulated Air-Dried Shallots.

Beef Salteñas
Makes 12

These meat-filled savories are a beloved midmorning snack in Bolivia. The dough of this delicacy is colored with ground annatto, an ingredient and dye used throughout Latin America.

2 cups all-purpose flour
2 tablespoons granulated sugar
¼ teaspoon fine sea salt
5 tablespoons unsalted butter
½ teaspoon ground annatto
½ cup boiling water
1 large egg yolk
Beef Filling (recipe follows)
12 pitted kalamata olives, halved
3 hard-cooked eggs, peeled and quartered lengthwise
1 large egg
1 teaspoon water

- In a large bowl, stir together flour, sugar, and salt.
- In a small saucepan, heat butter and annatto over medium heat until bubbly, approximately 2 minutes. Stir into flour mixture (mixture will be crumbly). Gradually stir in ½ cup boiling water. Stir in egg yolk.
- Turn out dough onto a lightly floured surface, and knead dough until smooth, approximately 2 minutes. Wrap dough in plastic wrap. Let stand at room temperature for 30 to 60 minutes, or refrigerate for up to 8 hours before using.
- Preheat oven to 425°. Line several rimmed baking sheets with parchment paper.
- Divide dough into 12 portions. On a lightly floured surface and using a rolling pin, roll out each dough portion to a 5½x4½-inch oval. Place 2 teaspoons Beef Filling, 2 olive halves, and 1 hard-cooked egg quarter in center of each dough oval.
- In a small bowl, whisk together 1 egg and 1 teaspoon water until foamy to make an egg wash. Brush egg wash onto edges of dough ovals. Fold dough ovals lengthwise over filling and press dough edges together to seal.
- Beginning at one end of each dough semicircle, fold over a corner of edge to make a small right angle. Continue folding over and crimping small portions of dough edge to achieve a braided look. Place salteñas, braided edges up, on prepared baking sheets. Freeze until firm, approximately 30 minutes.
- Brush salteñas with remaining egg wash.
- Bake until golden brown and heated through, 15 to 18 minutes. Serve warm.

MAKE-AHEAD TIP: Salteñas can be made ahead and frozen unbaked. Store in an airtight container with layers separated by parchment paper. Brush with egg wash and bake according to recipe.

Beef Filling
Makes approximately ¾ cup

Chuck steak cooked with a variety of vegetables and spices is a classic filling for salteñas.

2 teaspoons unflavored gelatin
1 cup beef stock, divided
2 teaspoons olive oil
2 ounces beef chuck steak, cut into ¼-inch cubes
2 tablespoons chopped yellow onion
2 tablespoons seeded and chopped yellow bell pepper
2 tablespoons frozen green peas
½ teaspoon smoked paprika
½ teaspoon dried oregano
¼ teaspoon ground cumin
¼ teaspoon fine sea salt
¼ teaspoon ground black pepper
3 ounces Yukon Gold potatoes, peeled and cut into ¼-inch cubes

- In a small bowl, stir together gelatin and ¼ cup beef stock until gelatin dissolves.
- In a heavy-bottom medium saucepan, heat oil over medium-high heat. Add beef; cook, stirring frequently, until browned, 2 to 3 minutes. Add onion, bell pepper,

peas, paprika, oregano, cumin, salt, and pepper; cook for approximately 2 minutes. Add remaining ¾ cup beef stock and potatoes; cook, uncovered, until potatoes are tender, approximately 10 minutes. Remove from heat and stir in gelatin mixture until it is dissolves. Refrigerate filling until set and thickened, 1 to 2 hours, stirring occasionally.

Pork & Shrimp Lumpia
Makes 12

Lumpia is a variation of spring rolls from the Philippines and can feature savory or sweet fillings. In this tea-appropriate version, ground pork and chopped shrimp are encased in the thin wrappers.

4 ounces ground pork
2 ounces uncooked shrimp, peeled, deveined, and finely chopped
¼ cup finely chopped green onion
2 tablespoons minced carrot
2 tablespoons chopped fresh parsley
¾ teaspoon sesame oil
½ teaspoon fine sea salt
½ teaspoon garlic powder
⅛ teaspoon ground black pepper
12 lumpia or spring roll wrappers*
1 large egg, lightly beaten
Vegetable oil, for frying
Prepared sweet and sour sauce, for serving

• In a large bowl, stir together pork, shrimp, onion, carrot, parsley, sesame oil, salt, garlic powder, and pepper. Cover and refrigerate for 30 minutes.
• Place 1 tablespoon pork mixture just below center of lumpia wrapper. (Cover remaining wrappers with a damp paper towel until ready to use.) Fold bottom of wrapper over filling. Brush remaining wrapper edges with beaten egg. Fold sides toward center over filling. Roll up lumpia tightly, pressing edge at end to seal. Repeat with remaining pork mixture and wrappers.
• In a large skillet, pour oil to a depth of 1 inch. Heat over medium heat until a deep-fry thermometer registers 350°. Fry lumpia, a few at a time, until golden brown, approximately 5 minutes, turning occasionally. Drain on paper towels. Serve immediately with sweet and sour sauce, if desired.

*Lumpia and spring roll wrappers can be found at any Asian grocery store.

Beef & Turnip Pasties
Makes 12

Pasties—pronounced PAHS-tees—are savory turnovers that are usually filled with meat and vegetables.

4 ounces beef filet, cut into ¼-inch cubes
¼ cup finely chopped, peeled Yukon gold potato
2 tablespoons finely chopped, peeled turnip
2 tablespoons finely chopped yellow onion
¾ teaspoon fine sea salt
¼ teaspoon ground pepper
1 large egg
1 tablespoon water
Pasty Dough (recipe follows)

- Preheat oven to 350°. Line a baking sheet with parchment paper.
- In a large bowl, stir together beef, potato, turnip, onion, salt, and pepper.
- In a small bowl, whisk together egg and 1 tablespoon water to make an egg wash.
- On a lightly floured surface, roll out dough to a ⅛-inch thickness. Using a 3½-inch round cutter, cut 12 rounds from dough.
- Place 1 tablespoon beef filling in the center of each dough circle. Using a pastry brush, lightly brush edges of dough circles with egg wash. Fold dough over to enclose filling, pressing out air and crimping dough edges with a fork dipped in flour. Transfer pasties to prepared baking sheet. Brush tops of pasties with egg wash.
- Bake for 25 minutes. Increase oven temperature to 375°, and bake until pasties are golden brown, 10 to 15 minutes more.

MAKE-AHEAD TIP: Pasties can be assembled and baked early in the day, cooled, placed in a single layer in a covered container, and refrigerated. Just before serving, place on a parchment-lined rimmed baking sheet and warm in a 350° oven for approximately 10 minutes.

Pasty Dough
Makes enough for 12 pasties

This easy, short dough is perfect for a meaty pasty filling. To keep the pastry flaky, be sure to handle the dough gently.

2 cups all-purpose flour
1 teaspoon fine sea salt
½ cup cold unsalted butter, diced
⅓ cup ice-cold water

- In a large bowl, whisk together flour and salt. Add butter and ⅓ cup water. Working gently with hands, mix ingredients together until a dough forms. Turn out dough onto a clean counter and knead until smooth and glossy, 6 to 10 minutes. Cover and refrigerate for at least 1 hour before using.

Deviled Tea Eggs
Makes 12

Infused with smoky Lapsang Souchong and with added flavor from Sriracha sauce and pickled ginger juice, these extraordinary deviled eggs take the typical luncheon staple to new heights.

6 large hard-cooked eggs
2½ cups water
⅓ cup gluten-free soy sauce
1 tablespoon light brown sugar
1½ tablespoons Lapsang Souchong black tea leaves*
⅓ cup mayonnaise
1 tablespoon minced shallot
1 tablespoon minced pickled ginger
½ tablespoon pickled ginger juice
1½ teaspoons Sriracha sauce
¼ teaspoon rice vinegar
⅛ teaspoon dry mustard
Garnish: pickled ginger and fresh chives

- Using the back of a spoon, gently tap eggs all over to crack shells, but do not peel.
- In a large saucepan, bring 2½ cups water, soy sauce, and brown sugar to a boil together over high heat, stirring until sugar dissolves. Add tea leaves and eggs; reduce heat to low. (If water does not completely cover eggs, add enough to do so.) Cover and simmer for 10 minutes; remove from heat. Uncover and let cool to room temperature.
- Transfer eggs and poaching liquid to a medium bowl. Cover and refrigerate for at least 2 hours. (The longer the eggs stand, the deeper the flavor and the more vibrant the marbling.)
- Peel eggs. Using a sharp knife, cut eggs in half lengthwise. Remove yolks from whites, and set whites aside.
- In a medium bowl, place yolks. Using a fork, mash yolks until very fine. Whisk in mayonnaise, shallot, ginger, ginger juice, Sriracha sauce, vinegar, and dry mustard.
- Transfer yolk mixture to a piping bag fitted with an open-star tip (Ateco #822). Pipe yolk mixture into egg white halves.
- Garnish with pickled ginger and chives, if desired.

*Lapsang Souchong is a heavily smoke-scented Chinese black tea.

MISCELLANEOUS SAVORIES | *Teatime Savories* 129

Teacup Salads
Makes 6 to 8 servings

Elegantly served in teacups, this enticing salad combines spring salad mix, fresh fruit, sliced almonds, blue cheese crumbles, and a fantastic dressing made of apple cider vinegar and Dijon mustard.

1 (5-ounce) package spring salad mix
1 cup fresh strawberries, hulled and sliced
1 cup fresh blueberries
¾ cup sliced almonds, lightly toasted
½ cup blue cheese crumbles
2 teaspoons apple cider vinegar
2 teaspoons Dijon mustard
1 teaspoon honey
½ teaspoon fine sea salt
¼ teaspoon ground black pepper
¼ cup extra-virgin olive oil

• In a large bowl, gently toss together salad mix, strawberries, blueberries, almonds, and blue cheese.
• In a small bowl, whisk together vinegar, mustard, honey, salt, and pepper. Gradually whisk in olive oil until emulsified. Pour vinaigrette over salad mixture, tossing gently to coat. Divide mixture among teacups. Serve immediately.

Quinoa-Stuffed Mushrooms
Makes 16

Tricolor quinoa, sweet potato, garlic, herbs, and fresh lemon juice stuffed inside portobello mushrooms yield healthful and flavorful bites that are ideal for vegans and enjoyable for those who aren't.

16 baby portobello mushrooms, cleaned and stemmed
2 teaspoons extra-virgin olive oil
¾ teaspoon fine sea salt, divided
⅓ cup tricolor quinoa
⅔ cup vegetable stock
½ cup mashed sweet potato
1 tablespoon pure olive oil
3 tablespoons minced shallots
2 cloves garlic, minced
2 teaspoons chopped fresh parsley
½ teaspoon chopped fresh oregano
½ teaspoon fresh lemon juice
⅛ teaspoon ground black pepper
Garnish: fresh oregano

• Preheat oven to 375°. Line a rimmed baking sheet with parchment paper.
• Arrange mushrooms stem side down on prepared baking sheet.

• Bake until liquid starts to release, 10 to 12 minutes. Let cool for 10 minutes. Transfer mushrooms to paper towels to absorb any extra liquid. Brush mushrooms with 2 teaspoons extra-virgin olive oil. Sprinkle with ½ teaspoon salt.
• In a medium saucepan, combine quinoa and stock; bring to a boil over medium heat. Reduce to medium-low heat. Cover and cook until quinoa is soft and translucent and stock is absorbed, 10 to 15 minutes. Transfer quinoa to a medium bowl. Stir in sweet potato.
• In a medium skillet, heat pure olive oil over medium heat. Add shallots and garlic, cooking until fragrant, approximately 1 minute. Stir shallot mixture, parsley, oregano, lemon juice, pepper, and remaining ¼ teaspoon salt into quinoa mixture until combined. Let cool slightly or to room temperature.
• Using a levered scoop slightly smaller than mushrooms, generously portion quinoa mixture into wells of each mushroom.
• Garnish with oregano, if desired. Serve warm or at room temperature.

Artichoke–Rice Salad in Bell Pepper Cups
Makes 8 servings

A tasty salad—made of white rice, artichoke hearts, and a lovely Lemon-Tarragon Vinaigrette—is housed in a nutritious bell pepper cup to create a unique and wholesome savory for teatime.

8 mini bell peppers (assorted colors)
2 cups cooked long-grain white rice
⅓ cup chopped canned artichoke hearts
Lemon-Tarragon Vinaigrette (recipe follows)
Garnish: fresh tarragon

• Using a sharp knife, cut off tops of bell peppers. Scoop out and discard seeds and membranes. If needed, trim bottoms of pepper cups so they sit level. Cover cups with damp paper towels, place in an airtight container, and refrigerate until needed. Chop trimmings and reserved tops to yield ⅓ cup chopped bell pepper.
• In a medium bowl, stir together rice, artichoke hearts, chopped bell pepper, and enough Lemon-Tarragon Vinaigrette to moisten. (Reserve remaining vinaigrette to drizzle on salad before serving.) Cover rice salad, and refrigerate until cold, approximately 4 hours.
• Place bell pepper cups on a serving dish, and fill with cold rice salad. Lightly drizzle with reserved vinaigrette. Serve immediately, or place in an airtight container and serve within 2 hours.
• Just before serving, garnish with fresh tarragon sprigs, if desired.

Lemon-Tarragon Vinaigrette
Makes ½ cup

This light dressing adds wonderful brightness to our Artichoke–Rice Salad in Bell Pepper Cups.

¼ cup rice vinegar
2 tablespoons extra-virgin olive oil
2 tablespoons fresh lemon juice
2 teaspoons finely minced shallot
1 teaspoon finely chopped fresh tarragon
½ teaspoon granulated sugar
½ teaspoon fine sea salt
¼ teaspoon ground black pepper

• In a small glass jar with a screw-top lid, combine rice vinegar, olive oil, lemon juice, shallot, tarragon, sugar, salt, and pepper, shaking well to emulsify.

MAKE-AHEAD TIP: Lemon-Tarragon Vinaigrette can be made a day in advance and refrigerated until needed. Let come to room temperature, and shake well to emulsify before serving.

Acknowledgments

EDITOR Lorna Reeves
CREATIVE DIRECTOR, LIFESTYLE
Melissa Sturdivant Smith
ART DIRECTOR Jodi Rankin Daniels
ASSOCIATE EDITOR Katherine Ellis
SENIOR COPY EDITOR Rhonda Lee Lother
EDITORIAL ASSISTANT Shelby Duffy
SENIOR PHOTOGRAPHER John O'Hagan
PHOTOGRAPHERS
Jim Bathie, Stephanie Welbourne Steele
CONTRIBUTING PHOTOGRAPHERS
William Dickey, Nicole Du Bois, Mac Jamieson,
Marcy Black Simpson
STYLIST Maghan Armstrong
CONTRIBUTING STYLISTS
Courtni Bodiford, Lucy Wilson
SENIOR DIGITAL IMAGE SPECIALIST Delisa McDaniel
TEST KITCHEN DIRECTOR Laura Crandall
FOOD STYLISTS/RECIPE DEVELOPERS
Aaron Conrad, Katie Moon Dickerson,
Kathleen Kanen, Vanessa Rocchio
CONTRIBUTING FOOD STYLISTS/RECIPE DEVELOPERS
Janet Lambert, Megan Lankford, Jade Sinacori,
Elizabeth Stringer, Irene Yeh

COVER
Photography by John O'Hagan
Styling by Maghan Armstrong
Food Styling by Aaron Conrad
Paragon *Rockingham Green* teapot and teacup and saucer set; Paragon *Golden Emblem (White)* cream soup bowl and saucer set, 2-tiered serving tray, and large sandwich tray; Meissen *Scattered Flowers* covered sugar bowl*.

TITLE PAGE
Page 2: Philippe Deshoulières *Coquine* teacup, tea saucer, dinner plate, and sugar bowl from BIA Cordon Bleu, 209-745-5685, *biacordonbleu.com*. Spode *Colonel Gray* salad plate, 12-inch oval serving platter, and 14-inch oval serving platter*. Sferra *Classico* tablecloth from Sferra, 877-336-2003, *sferra.com*.

MASTHEAD
Pages 4–5: Sadler (pattern unknown) teapot; Spode *Chelsea Garden* mini covered sugar bowl, creamer, and oval platter; Coalport *Maytime* dinner plate; Hammersley *Morgan Rose* dinner plate; and Winton *Summertime* square platter available for rent at Tea and Old Roses, 205-413-7753, *teaandoldroses.com*.

TABLE OF CONTENTS
Page 6: Noritake *Gardena* 16-inch oval serving platter; Anna Weatherley *Colours Celadon* dinner plate; Charles Field Haviland *Marjolaine* salad plate and flat cup and saucer set*.

INTRODUCTION
Page 9: Ralph Lauren China *Claire* teacup and saucer set, sugar bowl, and dinner plate; Oneida Silver *Clarette* salad fork*. Antique embroidered tablecloth from Hoover Antique Gallery, 205-822-9500, *hooverantiquegalleryal.com*. Martha Stewart cake stand from private collection.

TEA-STEEPING GUIDE
Page 10: Grace's Teaware *Crafted Gold Bee Lemon* teapot and teacup and saucer set from Gracie China Shop, *graciechinashop.com*. Royal Worcester *Howard Leather Green* 2-tiered serving tray*.

TEA-PAIRING GUIDE
Page 13: Haviland *Eden* flat cup and saucer set; Bernardaud *Sceaux* teapot; Haviland *Paradise* dinner plate and 12-inch chop plate*.

COMFORTING SOUPS
Page 14: Bernardaud *Brocante* dinner plate, creamer, sugar bowl, and teacup and saucer set from Bernardaud, 212-308-7835, *bernardaud.com/en/us*. Anna Weatherley *Anna's Palette Sky Blue* charger from Sasha Nicholas, 314-997-5854, *sashanicholas.com*. Christofle *Marly* dessert knife, dessert fork, and oval soup spoon; Raynaud *Polka White (Gold Trim)* footed cream soup bowl and saucer*. **Page 16:** Vera Wang for Wedgwood *Grosgrain* 5-piece place setting from Wedgwood, 877-720-3486, *wedgwoodusa.com*. **Page 17:** Wedgwood *Amherst* dinner plate, salad plate, teacup and saucer set, soup bowl and saucer, creamer, and covered sugar bowl; Westmoreland Silver *George & Martha Washington* soup spoon*. **Page 18:** Gien *Paris Paris* dessert plate; Gien *Filet Taupe* dinner plates, and teacup and saucer set from Yvonne Estelle's, 847-518-1232, *yvonne-estelles.com*. Le Creuset stackable ramekin from Le Creuset of America, 877-273-8738, *lecreuset.com*. Mikasa *French Countryside* 65-piece flatware set from Mikasa, 866-645-2721, *mikasa.com*. Tablecloth from Red and White Kitchen Company, 877-914-7440, *redandwhitekitchen.com*. **Page 19:** Paragon *First Love* dinner plate and fruit bowl; Shelley *Claire De Lune* salad plate; Alvin Silver *Chateau Rose* teaspoon*. **Page 20:** Noble Excellence *Twas the Night Before Christmas* salad plate; Gorham Silver *Strasbourg* youth 5 o'clock spoon*. Green bowl from Chantal, 800-365-4354, *chantal.com*. **Page 21:** Royal Doulton *Miramont* dinner plate; Wedgwood *Drury Lane* footed cream soup bowl and saucer set*. *Petite Meadow Green* tablecloth from Katherine Young Home, *katherineyounghome.com*. **Page 22:** Christian Dior *Tabriz* dinner plate, salad plate, teacup, and saucer*. *Colette* clear dessert bowl from Juliska, 843-974-8795, *juliska.com*. Linen hemstitch table runner in Cactus from Pottery Barn, 888-779-5176, *potterybarn.com*. **Page 23:** Coalport *Hong Kong* footed soup bowl and saucer set; Wood & Sons *Wincanton Blue and Rust* flat cup and saucer set and dinner plate; Herend *Princess Victoria Rust* covered sugar bowl; Reed & Barton *Spanish Baroque* round bowl soup spoon*. **Page 24:** Minton China *Minton Rose* dinner plate, salad plate, bread and butter plate*. Revol *Grand Classiques* 2.75-ounce lion head soup bowl from Sur La Table, 317-559-2041, *surlatable.com*. **Page 25:** Bernardaud *Brocante* dinner plate, creamer, sugar bowl, and teapot from Bernardaud, 212-308-7835, *bernardaud.com/en/us*. Anna Weatherley *Anna's Palette Sky Blue* charger from Sasha Nicholas, 314-997-5854, *sashanicholas.com*. Christofle *Marly* oval soup spoon; Raynaud *Polka White (Gold Trim)* footed cream soup bowl and saucer*. **Page 26:** Arte Italica *Perlina* cup and saucer; Philippe Deshoulières *Dhara* 5-piece place setting from Bromberg's, 205-749-6787, *brombergs.com*. **Page 28:** Royal Albert *Lady Carlyle* dinner plate, salad plate, bread and butter plate, and footed cream soup bowl and saucer; Wallace *Rose Point* sterling flatware*. **Page 29:** Kate Spade *Mercer Drive* 5-piece place setting from Lenox, 800-223-4311, *lenox.com*.

SCRUMPTIOUS QUICHES & PASTRIES
Page 30: Gien *Filet Taupe* dinner plates, creamer, covered sugar bowl, and teacup and saucer set from Yvonne Estelle's, 847-518-1232, *yvonne-estelles.com*. Barn *China Great White Collection* pedestal cake stand*. Tablecloth from Red and White Kitchen Company, 877-914-7440, *redandwhitekitchen.com*. **Page 32:** Coalport *Pageant* large sandwich tray*. **Page 33:** Ralph Lauren China *Claire* teapot, and teacup and saucer set*. Antique embroidered tablecloth from Hoover Antique Gallery, 205-822-9500, *hooverantiquegalleryal.com*. Martha Stewart cake stand from private collection. **Page 34:** Anna Weatherley *Colours Celadon* dinner plate; Charles Field Haviland *Marjolaine* salad plate*. **Page 35:** Teacup and saucer set (maker and pattern unknown), rectangular serving tray (maker and pattern unknown), and Americana Golden *Heritage* flatware available for rent from Tea and Old Roses, 205-413-7753, *teaandoldroses.com*. **Page 37:** Constanza *Vienna Celadon* dinner set from The Old World Emporium, *theoldworldemporium.com*. Stanley Roberts *Gold Valentine* salad fork*. **Page 39:** Ceralene *La Fayette* 15-inch oval platter, octagonal luncheon plate, and creamer*. **Page 40:** Gien *Filet Taupe* dinner plates, creamer, covered sugar bowl, and teacup and saucer set from Yvonne Estelle's, 847-518-1232, *yvonne-estelles.com*. Barn *China Great White Collection* pedestal cake stand*. Tablecloth from Red and White Kitchen Company, 877-914-7440, *redandwhitekitchen.com*. **Page 42:** Paragon *Golden Emblem (White)* 2-tiered serving tray*. **Page 43:** Wedgwood *Bianca* teapot and square handled cake plate; Mitterteich *Golden Lark* footed cup and saucer set; Kirk Stieff *Quadrille* sterling silver teaspoon*. **Page 44:** Bordallo Pinheiro *Cabbage Green* plate and 12-inch pedestal cake plate; Royal Doulton *Clovelly* salad plate and teacup and saucer*. **Page 45:** Royal Limoges *Nymphea Colibri* teapot, teacup, tea saucer, oval platter medium*. *Festival* tablecloth and *Farell* placemats from Sferra, 877-336-2003, *sferra.com*. **Page 46:** Haviland *The Princess* celery tray*. Carte Postale Vintage House tablecloth from HomeGoods, 800-888-0776, *homegoods.com*. **Page 47:** Spode *Colonel Gray* 12-inch oval serving platter*. **Page 48:** Spode *Trade Winds Blue* covered sugar bowl, salad plate gold trim, and 14-inch oval serving platter; Spode *Knightsbridge Cobalt Blue* dinner plate; Oneida Silver *Belmont-Lyons* salad fork*. White buffet tablecloth and place mats from World Market, 877-967-5362, *worldmarket.com*. **Page 50:** Wedgwood *Pashmina* 5-piece place setting from Wedgwood, 877-720-3486, *wedgwood.com*. West Elm gold flatware from West Elm, 888-922-4119, *westelm.com*. Kenaf natural table runner from Pottery Barn, 888-779-5176, *potterybarn.com*. **Page 52:** Gien *Millefleurs* oval platter from FX Dougherty, 800-834-3797, *fxdougherty.com*. **Page 53:** Oval platter from HomeGoods, 800-888-0776, *homegoods.com*. **Page 54:** Spode *Trade Winds Blue* teapot, salad plate gold trim, and square handled cake plate gold trim; Spode *Knightsbridge Cobalt Blue* dinner plate*. White buffet tablecloth and place mats from World Market, 877-967-5362, *worldmarket.com*. **Page 57:** Herend *Gwendolyn* teapot from Herend, *herendusa.com*. Annie Glass *Edgey Gold* round platter from Bromberg's, 205-871-3276, *brombergs.com*. Kim Seybert *Harlequin Plum* place mat from Kim Seybert, 704-949-2560, *kimseybert.com*.

TASTY TEA SANDWICHES
Page 58: Royal Albert 100 Years of Royal Albert *1940 English Chintz Duchess* 3-Piece Tea Set; Royal Albert *1900 Regency Blue* teacup and saucer 3-piece set from Wedgwood, 877-720-3486, *wedgwood.com/en-us*.

132 Teatime Savories | ACKNOWLEDGMENTS

Dainty Home Inc. tablecloth from HomeGoods, 800-888-0776, homegoods.com. **Page 60:** Bernardaud *Sceaux* teapot; Haviland *Paradise* dinner plate and 12-inch chop plate; Haviland *Eden* flat cup and saucer set*. **Page 61:** Sadler (pattern unknown) teapot; Spode *Chelsea Garden* mini covered sugar bowl and creamer; *Victoriana Rose* rectangular sandwich tray available for rent at Tea and Old Roses, 205-413-7753, teaandoldroses.com. **Page 62:** Bordallo Pinheiro *Cabbage Green* plate and dinner plate; Royal Doulton *Clovelly* teacup and saucer and teapot*. **Page 63:** Gien *Millefleurs* rectangular serving tray and 5-piece place setting from FX Dougherty, 800-834-3797, fxdougherty.com. **Page 64:** Royal Limoges *Arcade Grey and Gold* teapot, creamer, covered sugar bowl, dinner plate, and oval platter from BIA Cordon Bleu, 209-745-5685, biacordonbleu.com. Japan *Cellini Romanesque* flatware available for rent at Tea and Old Roses, 205-413-7753, teaandoldroses. com. **Page 65:** Royal Winton *Eleanor* Late Athena teapot; Royal Winton *Old Cottage Chintz* 14-inch oval serving platter*. **Page 66:** Ralph Lauren *Claire* teapot and oval serving platter*. Antique embroidered tablecloth from Hoover Antique Gallery, 205-822-9500, hooverantiquegalleryal.com. Martha Stewart cake stand from private collection. **Page 67:** Haviland *Louveciennes* 3-tiered tray*. **Page 68:** Constanza *Vienna Celadon* tea set and dinner set from The Old World Emporium, theoldworldemporium.com. **Page 71:** Royal Albert 100 Years of Royal Albert *1940 English Chintz Duchess* 3-Piece Tea Set; Royal Albert *1900 Regency Blue* teacup and saucer 3-piece set from Wedgwood, 877-720-3486, wedgwood.com/en-us. Dainty Home Inc. tablecloth from HomeGoods, 800-888-0776, homegoods.com. Oneida oval platter from private collection. **Page 73:** Minton *Ancestral* teacup and saucer set, round platter, creamer, and sugar bowl available for rent at Tea and Old Roses, 205-413-7753, teaandoldroses.com. Shelly *Dainty Pink* teapot*. **Page 74:** Coalport *Pageant* teapot, dinner plate, 12-inch chop plate, and large sandwich tray; Coalport *Athlone Blue* salad plate. Blue-and-white table overlay from private collection. **Page 76:** Barker Bros Ltd. *Dreamy* 3-tiered stand from The Brooklyn Teacup, 646-470-4344, thebrooklynteacup.com. French Bleu tablecloth from Fox and Brindle, foxandbrindle.com. **Page 77:** Noritake *Gardena* 16-inch oval serving platter; Anna Weatherley *Colours Celadon* dinner plate; Charles Field Haviland *Marjolaine* salad plate and flat cup and saucer set*. Vessels for flowers from Colliers Nursery, 205-822-3133, colliersnursery.com. **Page 78:** Royal Albert *Tranquillity* 3-tiered serving tray*. **Page 79:** Noble Excellence *Twas the Night Before Christmas* salad plate; Gorham Silver *Strasbourg* youth 5 o'clock spoon*. Green bowl from Chantal, 800-365-4354, chantal.com. **Page 80:** Royal Worcester *Howard Leather Green* 2-tiered serving tray*. **Page 81:** Herend *Chinese Bouquet Rust* 15-inch oval serving platter*. Tablecloth from HomeGoods, 800-888-0776, homegoods.com. **Page 82:** Spode *Colonel Gray* 12-inch oval serving platter and 14-inch oval serving platter*. **Page 83:** Royal Limoges *Nymphea Colibri* teapot and oval platter medium*. **Page 84:** Mottahedeh *Tobacco Leaf* teacup and saucer set from Mottahedeh, 800-443-8225, mottahedeh.com. White sandwich tray and vessel for centerpiece from HomeGoods, 800-888-0776, homegoods.com. **Page 85:** *Doily Lace* three-tier glass server from Fancy Flours, 406-587-0118, fancyflours.com. **Page 86:** Wedgwood *Hummingbird* 3-piece tea set, teacup and saucer set, 8-inch plate, and 13-inch oval platter from Wedgwood, 877-720-3486, wedgwood.com. **Page 89:** Gien *Millefleurs* 5-piece place setting and small square platter from FX Dougherty, 800-834-3797, fxdougherty.com.

DELECTABLE CANAPÉS & CROSTINI

Page 90: Sadler (pattern unknown) teapot; Spode *Chelsea Garden* mini covered sugar bowl, creamer, and oval platter available for rent at Tea and Old Roses, 205-413-7753, teaandoldroses.com. **Page 92:** Haviland *Louveciennes* 3-tiered tray and flat cup and saucer set*. **Page 93:** *Doily Lace* three-tier glass server from Fancy Flours, 406-587-0118, fancyflours.com. **Page 94:** Royal Albert *Tranquillity* dinner plate and dessert/pie plate*. **Page 95:** Minton *Ancestral* dinner plates available for rent at Tea and Old Roses, 205-413-7753, teaandoldroses.com. Shelly *Dainty Pink* teapot*. **Pages 96–97:** Sadler (pattern unknown) teapot; Spode *Chelsea Garden* mini covered sugar bowl and oval platter; Royal Chelsea *4377* teacup and saucer set; Royal Winton *Summertime* square platter available for rent at Tea and Old Roses, 205-413-7753, teaandoldroses.com. **Page 98:** Deshoulières *Coquine* dinner plate from BIA Cordon Bleu, 209-745-5685, biacordonbleu.com. Spode *Colonel Gray* salad plate, 12-inch oval serving platter, 14-inch oval serving platter*. **Page 99:** Herend *Chinese Bouquet Rust* 15-inch oval serving platter*. **Page 102:** Anna Weatherley *Colours Celadon* dinner plate; Charles Field Haviland *Marjolaine* salad plate*. **Page 103:** Haviland *Paradise* dinner plate; Bernardaud *Sceaux* oval serving platter; Haviland *Eden* flat cup and saucer set; Christfole France *Spatours* spoon*. **Page 104:** Barker Bros Ltd. *Dreamy* 3-tiered stand from The Brooklyn Teacup, 646-470-4344, thebrooklynteacup.com. **Page 105:** Haviland *Paradise* dinner plate; Christole France *Spatours* dessert fork*. **Page 106:** Annieglass *Ruffle* oval platter from Annieglass, 888-761-0050, annieglass.com. Royal Crown Derby *Elizabeth Gold* 5-piece place setting and teapot from Bromberg's Inc., 205-871-3276, brombergs.com. Beaded place mat from Z Gallerie, 877-779-4255, zgallerie.com. **Page 107:** Royal Limoges *Nymphea Colibri* dinner plate*. **Page 108:** Gien *Paris Paris* dessert plate; and Gien *Filet Taupe* dinner plates from Yvonne Estelle's, 847-518-1232, yvonne-estelles.com. Le Creuset stackable ramekin from Le Creuset of America, 877-273-8738, lecreuset.com. **Page 109:** Ralph Lauren China *Claire* teacup and saucer set and dinner plate*. Antique embroidered tablecloth from Hoover Antique Gallery, 205-822-9500, hooverantiquegalleryal.com. Martha Stewart cake stand from private collection. **Page 110:** Royal Winton *Old Cottage Chintz* 14-inch oval serving platter*. **Page 111:** Bernardaud *Prunus* teapot and creamer; Bernardaud *Capucine* oval platter and saucer from Bernardaud, 212-308-7835, bernardaud.com/en/us. **Page 112:** [Top] Royal Heidelberg *A1029* dinner plate*. [Bottom] Wedgwood *Hummingbird* dinner plate*. **Page 113:** Constanza *Vienna Celadon* dinner set from The Old World Emporium, theoldworldemporium.com. **Page 114:** George Borgfeldt *BOG78* serving plate from private collection. **Page 115:** *Doily Lace* three-tier glass server from Fancy Flours, 406-587-0118, fancyflours.com.

MISCELLANEOUS SAVORIES GALORE

Page 116: Haviland *Imperatrice Eugenie* teapot and flat cup and saucer set; Reed & Barton *Grande Renaissance* modern hollow knife and teaspoon*. **Page 118:** Tasting glasses for shrimp salads from Pier 1, pier1.com.

Page 119: Royal Limoges *Arcade Grey and Gold* dinner plate and teacup and saucer from BIA Cordon Bleu, 209-745-5685, biacordonbleu.com. **Page 120:** *Rufolo Glass Gold* two-tiered tray from Vietri, 919-245-4180, vietri.com. **Page 121:** Spode *Trade Winds Blue* salad plate gold trim; Spode *Knightsbridge Cobalt Blue* dinner plate*. White buffet tablecloth and place mats from World Market, 877-967-5362, worldmarket.com. **Page 122:** Royal Worcester *Howard Leather Green* 2-tiered serving tray*. **Page 123:** Minton *Ancestral* teacup and saucer set and medium oval platter available for rent at Tea and Old Roses, 205-413-7753, teaandoldroses.com. **Page 125:** *Capucine* oval platter from Bernardaud, 212-308-7835, bernardaud.com/en/us. **Page 128:** Barker Bros Ltd. *Dreamy* 3-tiered stand from The Brooklyn Teacup, 646-470-4344, thebrooklynteacup.com. **Page 129:** Mottahedeh *Tobacco Leaf* teacup and saucer set and octagonal tray from Mottahedeh, 800-443-8225, mottahedeh.com. Reed & Barton *Burgundy* salad fork*. **Page 130:** [Left] Royal Doulton *Monteigne* dinner plate; Bernardaud *Myosotis* teacup and saucer set*. [Right] Spode *Savoy White* square cake plate*. **Page 131:** Bordallo Pinheiro *Cabbage Green* large dinner plate*.

END PAGE

Bernardaud *Sceaux* teapot; Haviland *Paradise* creamer; Haviland *Eden* flat cup*.

BACK COVER

Photography by Jim Bathie
Styling by Lucy Wilson
Food Styling by Janet Lambert
Gien *Millefleurs* rectangular serving tray and 5-piece place setting from FX Dougherty, 800-834-3797, fxdougherty.com.

*from Replacements, Ltd., 800-737-5223, replacements.com.

EDITOR'S NOTE: All items not listed are from private collections and no further information is available.

NOTABLE TEA PURVEYORS

- The Boulder Tea Company, 303-817-7057, bouldertea.co
- The East Indies Tea Company, 717-228-2000, eastindiescoffeeandtea.com
- Elmwood Inn Fine Teas, 800-765-2139, elmwoodinn.com
- Harney & Sons, 888-427-6398, harney.com
- Joseph's Tea, 352-679-1339, josephstea.com
- The Larkin Tea Company, 304-707-0142, larkintea.com
- Simpson & Vail, 800-282-8327, svtea.com
- Tea by Two, 410-838-6811, shop.teabytwo.com
- Tea-For-All, 609-577-8038, tea-for-all.com
- The Tea Shoppe, 304-413-0890, theteashoppewv.com

Recipe Index

BEEF
Beef & Turnip Pasties 128
Beef Filling 126
Beef-Mushroom Carbonnade in Pastry Shells 46
Beef Salteñas 126
Creole Filet Tea Sandwiches 72
Garden Vegetable, Roast Beef & Cheddar Tea Sandwiches 78
Pastrami-Avocado Tea Sandwiches 83
Reuben Swirls 50
Roast Beef Croissants 65
Roast Beef Pastries 49
Roast Beef–Radish Tea Sandwiches 89
Roast Beef, Tomato & Cheese Tea Sandwiches 70
Watercress Pesto & Steak Crostini 99

CHEESE
Apple, Hazelnut & Cacao Nib Triple-Stack Tea Sandwiches 82
Arugula-Pecan Pesto & Goat Cheese Tea Sandwiches 72
Assam-Vegetable Tartlets 52
Baked Ham & Cheese Sliders 79
Beet Hummus Frico Cups 123
Champagne & Tarragon Radish Flower Canapés 107
Chicken Cordon Bleu Pastry Swirls 45
Chicken Cordon Bleu Salad on Croissants 85
Creamy Celery & Blue Cheese Triple-Stack Sandwiches 80
Cucumber & Mint Cream Cheese Pinwheels 70
Cucumber–Herbed Cheese Tea Sandwiches 62
Garden Vegetable, Roast Beef & Cheddar Tea Sandwiches 78
Heirloom Tomato Tart 44
Herbed Goat Cheese 125
Honeydew, Coppa & Feta Canapés 112
Lamb Puff Pastry Roulades 38
Mascarpone-Broccoli Soup 22
Mini Smoked Salmon, Gruyère & Herb Frittatas 36
Muffaletta Palmiers 56
Petite Ham & Cheese Quiches 38
Petite Savory Éclairs 125
Pork & Mole Crostini 98
Reuben Swirls 50
Roast Beef Pastries 49
Roast Beef, Tomato & Cheese Tea Sandwiches 70
Salmon Petits Toasts 115
Savory Gruyère Palmiers 46

Savory Lobster Cheesecakes 120
Smoked Fish Toasts 104
Smoked Salmon & Caper Cream Cheese–Filled Cucumber Canapés 102
Smoked Salmon & Pickled Okra Roll-Ups 87
Soupe à l'Oignon 18
Strawberry & Goat Cheese Crostini 92
Teacup Salads 130
Turkey-Swiss Roulades 65

CONDIMENTS & SPREADS
Avocado-Lemon Spread 83
Creamy Horseradish-Dill Sauce 109
Creole Mustard Butter 73
Herbed Aïoli 97
Lemon-Chive Rémoulade 95
Lemon-Dill Aïoli 93, 108
Lemon-Lime Vinaigrette 106
Lemon-Tarragon Vinaigrette 131
Lemon-Thyme Vinaigrette 123
Niçoise Olive Tapenade 115
Pistachio-Mint Pesto 69
Russian Dressing 51
Savoury Aïoli 79
Sour Cream–Horseradish Aïoli 89
Watercress Pesto 99
White Wine Vinaigrette 119

CRUST & DOUGH
Assam Tartlet Shells 53
Pasty Dough 128

EGG
Asparagus-Pancetta Quiche 36
Asparagus-Topped Frittata Bites 42
Beef Salteñas 126
Black Forest Ham Quiches 35
Caramelized Leek & Pancetta Quiche 33
Curried Egg Salad Canapés 97
Deviled Tea Eggs 129
Egg & Cress Tea Sandwiches 78
Ham-and-Egg Salad Tea Sandwiches 62
Herbed Deviled Eggs 119
Mini Smoked Salmon, Gruyère & Herb Frittatas 36
Mini Zucchini Quiches 34
Mushroom-Leek Quiche Squares 32
Omelet & Asparagus Canapés 93
Petite Ham & Cheese Quiches 38
Quiche Lorraine 40

FRUIT
Apple, Hazelnut & Cacao Nib Triple-Stack Tea Sandwiches 82
Bannann Peze with Quick Pikliz 124

Carrot-Apple Soup 16
Cranberry-Walnut Ham Salad Tea Sandwiches 80
Curried Shrimp & Mango Salad Tea Sandwiches 67
Date & Roasted Chicken Salad Tea Sandwiches 66
Ham & Pineapple Pinwheels 67
Heirloom Tomato Tart 44
Honeydew, Coppa & Feta Canapés 112
Lemony Couscous-Shrimp Salad 122
Lobster Salad Tea Sandwiches 89
Pastrami-Avocado Tea Sandwiches 83
Roast Beef, Tomato & Cheese Tea Sandwiches 70
Shrimp Salsa Cups 55
Strawberry & Goat Cheese Crostini 92
Teacup Salads 130
Tomato-Artichoke Bruschetta Phyllo Cups 52
Tomato-Basil Soup 20

LAMB
Lamb Puff Pastry Roulades 38
Roast Lamb Salad Tea Sandwiches with Pistachio-Mint Pesto 69

PORK
Asparagus & Ham Tartines 108
Asparagus-Pancetta Quiche 36
Baked Ham & Cheese Sliders 79
Black Forest Ham Quiches 35
Butternut Squash Tartlets 51
Caramelized Leek & Pancetta Quiche 33
Chicken Cordon Bleu Pastry Swirls 45
Chicken Cordon Bleu Salad on Croissants 85
Cranberry-Walnut Ham Salad Tea Sandwiches 80
Ham-and-Egg Salad Tea Sandwiches 62
Ham & Pineapple Pinwheels 67
Honeydew, Coppa & Feta Canapés 112
Honey Ham & Dijon Tea Sandwiches 76
Jambalaya Tartlets 56
Muffaletta Palmiers 56
Petite Ham & Cheese Quiches 38
Pork & Mole Crostini 98
Pork & Shrimp Lumpia 127
Prosciutto & Artichoke Herbed Crostini 97
Prosciutto, Pesto & Black-Eyed Pea Hummus Tea Sandwiches 64
Quiche Lorraine 40
Roast Pork Salad Mini Phyllo Cups 41
Roasted Butternut Squash Soup with Crispy Prosciutto 23
Seared Scallop & Chorizo Canapés with Herb Sauce 100

POULTRY
Chicken & Artichoke Salad Tea Sandwiches 86
Chicken Cordon Bleu Pastry Swirls 45
Chicken Cordon Bleu Salad on Croissants 85
Darjeeling-Poached Chicken Salad Sandwiches 85
Date & Roasted Chicken Salad Tea Sandwiches 66
Duck Salad Brioche Sandwiches 60
Earl Grey Chicken Salad Tea Sandwiches 61
Jambalaya Tartlets 56
Turkey-Swiss Roulades 65

SEAFOOD & FISH
Chilled Crab Salad Sandwiches 74
Clam Chowder 29
Crab Cake Crostini 94
Crab Tea Sandwiches 76
Curried Shrimp & Mango Salad Tea Sandwiches 67
Fish Taquitos with Creamy Slaw 100
Jambalaya Tartlets 56
Lemon-Lime Scallop Canapés 106
Lemony Couscous-Shrimp Salad 122
Lobster Salad Tea Sandwiches 89
Lobster "Spring Roll" Tea Sandwiches 75
Mini Smoked Salmon, Gruyère & Herb Frittatas 36
Pork & Shrimp Lumpia 127
Prawn Salad Tea Sandwiches 70
Salmon Petits Toasts 115
Salmon Rillettes 103
Salmon Roses on Cucumber Rounds 94
Savory Lobster Cheesecakes 120
Seared Scallop & Chorizo Canapés with Herb Sauce 100
Shrimp Bisque 28
Shrimp Salsa Cups 55
Shrimp Stock 122
Shrimp-Topped Avocado & Cucumber Microgreen Salads 118
Smoked Fish Toasts 104
Smoked Salmon & Caper Cream Cheese–Filled Cucumber Canapés 102
Smoked Salmon & Pickled Okra Roll-Ups 87
Smoked Salmon Blini 108
Smoked Salmon–Cucumber Canapés with Niçoise Olive Tapenade 115

TEA-INFUSED
Assam Tartlet Shells 53
Assam-Vegetable Tartlets 52
Darjeeling-Poached Chicken Salad Sandwiches 85

Deviled Tea Eggs 129
Earl Grey Chicken Salad Tea Sandwiches 61

TOPPINGS
Buttered Croutons 19
Edible Whole-Grain Spoons 26
Leaf Crackers 22
Quick Pikliz 124
Star Croutons 20

VEGAN
Artichoke–Rice Salad in Bell Pepper Cups 131
Arugula Salad 41
Bannann Peze with Quick Pikliz 124
Curried Red Lentil–Carrot Soup 21
Quick Pikliz 124
Quinoa-Stuffed Mushrooms 130

VEGETABLES
Artichoke–Rice Salad in Bell Pepper Cups 131
Arugula-Pecan Pesto & Goat Cheese Tea Sandwiches 72
Arugula Salad 41
Asparagus & Ham Tartines 108
Asparagus-Pancetta Quiche 36
Asparagus-Topped Frittata Bites 42
Assam-Vegetable Tartlets 52
Bannann Peze with Quick Pikliz 124
Beanie Flatbread Hummus Bites 110
Beef-Mushroom Carbonnade in Pastry Shells 46
Beef & Turnip Pasties 128
Beet Hummus Frico Cups 123
Butternut Squash Tartlets 51
Caramelized Leek & Pancetta Quiche 33
Carrot-Apple Soup 16
Cauliflower-Leek Soup 19
Champagne & Tarragon Radish Flower Canapés 107
Chicken & Artichoke Salad Tea Sandwiches 86
Chilled Sweet Pea Soup 24
Creamy Celery & Blue Cheese Triple-Stack Sandwiches 80
Cucumber & Mint Cream Cheese Pinwheels 70
Cucumber Canapés with Dilled Butter 114
Cucumber–Herbed Cheese Tea Sandwiches 62
Cucumber-Radish Canapés 112
Cucumber-Tarragon Fleur-de-Lis Canapés 104
Cucumber-Watercress Canapés 113
Curried Red Lentil–Carrot Soup 21

Egg & Cress Tea Sandwiches 78
Fish Taquitos with Creamy Slaw 100
Garden Vegetable, Roast Beef & Cheddar Tea Sandwiches 78
Golden Beet Soup 16
Heirloom Tomato Tart 44
Loaded Potato Twists 121
Lobster Salad Tea Sandwiches 89
Lobster "Spring Roll" Tea Sandwiches 75
Mascarpone-Broccoli Soup 22
Mini Zucchini Quiches 34
Mushroom-Leek Quiche Squares 32
Omelet & Asparagus Canapés 93
Pastrami-Avocado Tea Sandwiches 83
Pork & Mole Crostini 98
Prosciutto & Artichoke Herbed Crostini 97
Prosciutto, Pesto & Black-Eyed Pea Hummus Tea Sandwiches 64
Quick Pikliz 124
Quinoa-Stuffed Mushrooms 130
Radish & Herbed Butter Sandwiches 74
Roast Beef–Radish Tea Sandwiches 89
Roast Beef, Tomato & Cheese Tea Sandwiches 78
Roasted Butternut Squash Soup with Crispy Prosciutto 23
Salmon Roses on Cucumber Rounds 94
Shrimp Salsa Cups 55
Shrimp-Topped Avocado & Cucumber Microgreen Salads 118
Smoked Salmon & Caper Cream Cheese–Filled Cucumber Canapés 102
Smoked Salmon & Pickled Okra Roll-Ups 87
Smoked Salmon–Cucumber Canapés with Niçoise Olive Tapenade 115
Soupe à l'Oignon 18
Springtime Vegetable Tartlets 42
Tarragon & Cucumber Flower Canapés 110
Teacup Salads 130
Tomato-Artichoke Bruschetta Phyllo Cups 52
Tomato-Basil Soup 20
Watercress Cream Soup 24
Watercress Pesto & Steak Crostini 99
Wild Mushroom and Chestnut Soup 26

EDITOR'S NOTE: Recipes listed in gold are gluten-free, provided gluten-free versions of processed ingredients such as condiments, precooked meat, stocks, and toppings are used.